A WELL-SPICED LIFE

*An exuberant discovery of Sephardic food
and faith*

Barbara Bensoussan

Praise for A Well-Spiced Life

This is so much more than a cookbook. Barbara Bensoussan takes us on a journey through life, seen through the prism of a pot bubbling on the stove. With candor, ebullience, and wry humor, she shares her sojourn from bagels to bourekas, her thoughts on all things culinary, and a smorgasbord of lively vignettes. A treat for both body and soul.

--Bassi Gruen, former chief editor, *Family First* magazine

Barbara Bensoussan, famed columnist in Mishpacha Magazine, expresses her life's narrative with cooking and other life experiences, by weaving two worlds into one. Her passion for Sephardic cooking and expression of Sephardic Judaism are apparent in this masterpiece. This book is a must-read and truly original.

--Yehuda Azoulay, Founder of Sephardic Legacy Series/Institute for Preserving Sephardi Heritage

This book is much more than a recipe collection. It's an evocative and entertaining journey filled with colorful characters and scenes. Barbara brings her family, friends, and culture to life as she shares the secret techniques of the food that brings them all together. The recipes are good, but the read might be even better.

--Shana Friedman, editor, *Mishpacha Magazine*

In her signature upbeat style, Barbara describes her delicious adventure into the world of Sephardic cooking and culture.

The recipes are simple to follow, and I enjoyed the description of the spices that make Sephardic cooking so colorful and tasty.
--Estee Kafra, cookbook author and blogger

Barbara combines the rich aromas and flavors of a "mixed" Jewish marriage. Between her wise and very funny observations on the ins and outs of East meeting West, she shares a treasure of Jewish wisdom peppered with exotic but traditional Sephardic cuisine. Delicious reading!
--Yaffa Ganz, beloved Jewish children's author and essayist

Dedicated to my mother, Mrs. Gladys Greenfield, an intrepid American-
Jewish cook who got me started in the kitchen, and passed on her enthusiasm for intriguing new recipes. . .

...and my mother-in-law, a"h, Mrs. Gisele Bensoussan, a formidable Moroccan cook who so generously spent many hours passing on her culinary expertise to her eager daughter-in-law.

Contents

Introduction

**From Bagels to Bourekas: The Evolution of my
Sephardic Family Table**

There is a famous Yiddish saying that says: Man plans, and
God laughs. Well, He certainly got a good laugh out of me.

I grew up in the 1960's in the mother of all suburbs, Levittown. We were a second-generation Jewish family, and most of
the adults were teachers and professors. We were proud to be
all-American, but on the occasional Jewish holiday or Friday
evening, we were prone in indulge in a bit of Religion Lite. I
grew up assuming that I too would grow up to be a professor,
take my religion Lite, and, like my dear old Mum, marry a Nice
Jewish Boy from New York.

But that's not how things turned out, oh no.

Somehow I have ended up married to a Nice Jewish Boy
not from New York but from Casablanca; I no longer take my
religion Lite, but full strength; I became a writer instead of a
professor, and I have, *kenahora*, six (yes, six!) darling children.

So how did I end up this way, much to the dismay of my

family? How did I end up living in the Holy City of Brooklyn, amidst Orthodox men in black hats and women in custom wigs? How did I end up, at my high school's twenty-year reunion, finding that my claim to fame was that I'd had more kids than anybody else? And to top it all off, how did I end up in the middle of a Moroccan family that remains scattered between Casablanca, Israel and France?

My young- adult visions of myself ensconced in a little college town teaching undergraduates and browsing in Barnes & Noble has given way to a life that is considerably more rich, diverse, and family-centered. As I moved from all-American Jewish girl to a Sephardic, observant Jewish wife and mother, I found myself obliged to assimilate, in addition to the American suburban culture of my youth, any number of new cultural perspectives: Moroccan culture, French culture, Israeli culture, Syrian and other Sephardic cultures, Orthodox Ashkenazic culture and that peculiar animal known as New York culture. And as I sat in Brooklyn with all these different waves of culture washing around me, and a family of eight to feed, guess what? I learned lots and lots about Jewish food, especially its Sephardic permutations.

The Gentle Persuasions of Shabbat

I have another famous Jewish saying that has shaped my life. It goes like this: Shabbos keeps the Jews as much as the Jews keep Shabbos. Keeping the Seventh Day holy is not just an archaic Biblical commandment; it's G-d's gift of a universal pause button.

During the whole of my childhood, Saturday was just that, no more and no less, the first day of the weekend. As I was growing up in the suburbs of Philadelphia, my parents' idea of a good Jewish way to spend Saturday morning was to drive into

Northeast Philly and take the family to a really good-sized public library. There, after spending an hour stocking up on armloads of books, we would drive across the street to pick up bagels and lox at the bagel bakery for Sunday morning. The bagels were definitely on the *Jewish* track, and so were the books for that matter, but they were still a long ways from being *Shabbos*.

In high school and college, Friday nights meant there were parties to go to, typically boisterous, crowded affairs where it was *de rigueur* to include kegs of beer, music blasting so loud we shouted to be heard, and whatever shenanigans went along with way too much beer and adolescent high energy. I went along to these things often enough, mostly for lack of other social alternatives, but deep down I *knew* there must be a better way. Maybe dinner parties for six or eight? A hike in the woods with a few close friends? And what self-respecting Jewish person wouldn't have preferred outrageous quantities of good food to outrageous quantities of cheap beer?

Eventually, halfway through my career in graduate school, a friend pulled me into a weekly class about Judaism with an Orthodox rabbi. Having grown up thinking Orthodox Jews (or any true believers, for that matter) must necessarily be close-minded, simple-minded, and hopelessly mired in some kind of medieval theological muck, I was put off to find myself confronting a teacher who was shrewd, insightful, and seemed to understand an awful lot more about my world than I did about his. It didn't take long for me to figure out that Judaism was much richer, deeper, and intellectually sophisticated than anything I'd learned in the Sunday school of my family's Reform synagogue ("that *Reform school*," as my more traditional grandmother used to call it, as she harangued my father: "Are you still sending your kids to Reform school?").

But the rabbi knew that Judaism is not meant to be purely

an intellectual exercise; it's meant to be *lived,* and cannot be fully appreciated if only observed from the sidelines. He and some newly religious friends of mine began to insist that I "come for Shabbos." I began to accept their invitations when my schedule permitted. At my friends' place, Shabbos was a pleasant break from the rigors of graduate school: a day of nice family meals and catching up with close friends, lots of sleep, pleasure reading, and playing with their baby. At the rabbi's house, where there was a small army of little kids, Shabbos was joyous and rambunctious, if materially more austere: scarce furnishings, plain food, portraits of somber-looking rabbis on the walls and bookshelves filled with massive Hebrew tomes. I liked it there too, although never in my wildest imagination could I imagine myself becoming the least bit like these people. The rabbi's wife was very sweet and pretty, and no dummy either, yet she had a simplicity that I just couldn't fathom and only later came to appreciate as the product of an upbringing unmarred by conflict, doubts, or existential crises. Everybody *I* knew was busily, narcissistically wrapped up in their Woody Allen-style personal conflicts over twisted family dynamics and gender politics and lofty career ambitions.

The rabbi encouraged me strongly to go learn more about Judaism in Israel. "You'll never grow if you stay in Ann Arbor," he said, and I felt mildly resentful at the implied criticism of the academic world I thought so cosmopolitan. My friend gave me a brochure about a summer learning program at Neve Yerushalayim Yeshiva for women in Jerusalem: they were giving away scholarships that offered plane fare, room, board and tuition for two months for a mere six hundred dollars. Since I am a person enamored of both travel and a good bargain, it was exactly the kind of offer I couldn't refuse. Several weeks later, I was pleasantly surprised to find myself selected for a teaching award. The prize? Seven hundred dollars. Heaven had deposited the money directly into my lap, the six hundred bucks plus spending money.

I took that as a sign to pack my bags. Now, I wasn't so sure I wanted to spend two months in a place they called a *yeshiva*. On the other hand, I reasoned, it was only for two months, and no one was going to chain me to my chair. If nothing else, it would be a cheap opportunity to go to Israel for the first time. So with a certain amount of trepidation, and some excitement as well, I signed away my prize money and my summer vacation.

Getting Holy in the Holy Land

Suffice it to say that it ended up being an eye-opening and soul-opening summer, difficult and exhilarating at the same time as I struggled, sometimes kicking and screaming, to see things from Orthodox Judaism's diametrically different point of view, to absorb new words and concepts, to see my modern ideas clash with a world-view that was so much older and wiser than my own. The city of Jerusalem itself was a revelation: the holiness that even my cynicism-encrusted soul managed to sense at the Western Wall, the beauty of the city's crumbling white stone, lit up rose and gold at sunrise and sunset; the odd combination of practicality and mysticism among its inhabitants. I went to the Wall and cried; I went to Yad V'Shem and cried; I prayed alone on a hilltop near the yeshiva and cried, feeling that Jerusalem was cracking open something that had been closed inside me all my life. And yet there was intense joy in all of this too: wonderful friends, college dorm-type discussions late into the night, sightseeing trips around that astonishing little country; a wedding in Modi'in where Rabbi Shlomo Carlebach officiated, chanting for what seemed like hours to an enraptured band of arty-looking followers of every conceivable size, shape and color, clothed in gauzy flowing Indian-print clothing and sandals.

It was an eye- and soul-opening summer, and it was a heart-opening summer as well; during my last week in Israel, when I was in one of my defiant moods and feeling sick and tired of the yeshiva, I ran off with a friend to Netanya where the good Lord, in his infinite mercy and wisdom, put my future husband right into my path. We stumbled upon each other near the beach and struck up a conversation that lasted all day, then all week, and now over twenty years later, fortunately, most of the time we're still talking to each other!

(For many years I wondered why the Master of the Universe apparently chose to reward rather than punish my rebellious flight from the yeshiva. Then I realized that He had actually allowed Himself the last laugh; He sent me a person who would come to demand nothing less than the highest Jewish standards for our family!)

By the time I got on the plane to come home, I had acquired too strong a taste for Torah Judaism to let it slide. I resolved to keep up kashruth and Shabbos as best I could back in the U.S. And of course there was the potential of a future with that tall, dark and handsome Sephardi boy I had met in Netanya...

O Brave New World!

When I met my husband-to-be he was visiting his parents in Israel, who'd retired there from Morocco. But it turned out that he really lived in Strasbourg, France. He persuaded me to visit him there the following December, where I was able to get to know not only him but most of his family. His older, married brothers were religious, and given my own new commitment to observance it was easy to blend in with everybody.

But now I saw a whole new type of Shabbos—er, *Shabbat*,

as my Sephardic family-to-be now said. I mean, it was still a day of rest, and family time, and praying time and eating time—but the *food!* O Brave New World! No more solitary matzoh balls floating lonely as a cloud in a bowl of watery chicken soup! No more gefilte fish stained scarlet with horseradish or mushy cholent for lunch!

Here were arrays of colorful salads, carrots and beets and peppers and eggplant; slices of trout napped with spicy red sauce; meats stewed with vegetables or fruits. I had never had occasion to taste Moroccan food before, and it was a revelation; everything was lovely to look at and sang with flavor on the tongue. Now *that* was a culture worth marrying into!

And so, gentle reader, I married him. We became one of those "mixed" marriages. Actually, since according to Jewish law a wife assumes the customs of her husband's family, my husband still takes delight in announcing to people that he "converted" me. But here, eventually, the last laugh was on him, for he ended up following me to America, and we settled in a predominantly Ashkenazic neighborhood. There, once he got his American citizenship, he could frequently be heard to proclaim to any interested listeners that, having been born in North Africa, he had just become a bona fide Afro-American.

The truth is that "mixed" marriages are not for everyone. Despite the fact that I had learned a serviceable French in high school and college, which was tremendously helpful for integrating into my husband's family, there were still many significant differences in expectations and culture that required considerable flexibility to negotiate. In fact, over twenty years later, the learning curve has not yet leveled off completely.

Moroccans, for example, tend to be very *bon vivant*; they like to dress with style, embellish their homes with flair, and entertain with sumptuous, beautifully presented food. They are generous and sociable to a fault; they will entertain and give gifts lavishly even when they can't afford to, because it would be humiliating to be perceived as stingy or poor. Ditto for offering favors they may or may not be in a position to fulfill; it would be shameful to refuse an appeal for help. The concept of "needing one's personal space" makes no sense to a Moroccan, because he is happiest when surrounded nonstop with friends and family.

Both men and women from Morocco tend to be very traditional. Since women living in an Arab country were not able to work outside the home, Jewish housewives channeled their drive for achievement into running spotless, well-organized homes, making extravagant meals, and taking care of their husbands and children. In fact, the Moroccan wife's chief pride is showing she ought to win the prize for the most attentive and solicitous spouse and mother, with a bathtub so clean you could eat her gourmet dinners right off the bottom. Unlike American women, who wage bitter wars with their spouses over who will vacuum the living room or bathe the kids, a model Moroccan wife refuses to let her husband worry about the housework or young children, because after all, he is so very pressured and busy earning a living for the family [usually true, by the way; the model Moroccan Jewish husband also works very hard]. The typical Sephardic male's way of "helping" in the house, therefore, is to stuff a few bills into his wife's hand and enjoin her to go hire a cleaning lady.

Similarly, while a Sephardic male may be very invested in the quality of the food he eats, he rarely expects to get involved in making it. Since I like to cook and don't do well with people underfoot, I never had a problem with this. Besides, when my husband and I first got married, I knew how to cook—or *thought* I did. I was able to make American-style meals (meaning a smattering of dishes culled from American and Italian and Chinese recipes), for small groups of people. But I didn't know the least thing about cooking *Moroccan* food or cooking for more than a few people. We had moved to Boro Park, a Chasidic neighborhood in Brooklyn, and there I was immediately thrown into yet a different kind of culture shock. . .

Kitchen Evolution

In Boro Park I encountered people with dining room tables that seated twenty, and who served fifteen people every night for supper when there *weren't* any guests. When I went out to buy a frying pan, choosing something about the right size to make an omelette, I found myself next in line to a hefty Boro Park matron buying an industrial-sized stock pot and the largest frying pan I'd ever seen. Obviously, with the addition of one after the other little bundles of joy, my sense of proportions grew larger, and those industrial-sized stockpots began to look just about the right size—if not maybe a bit on the *small* side...

(An aside: this certainly gave me a new perspective on the fuss the media makes every year about producing Thanksgiving dinners for little American families. What's so hard about throwing a turkey in the oven to roast? Those "cooking experts" should take a guided tour of Boro Park, where indefatigable *balabustas* churn out five-course dinners for twelve every Friday afternoon, with toddlers winding in between their feet and husbands rushing in wanting lunch in ten seconds flat.)

As the years went by, and we had many visits from my husband's family, I was able to build up a repertoire of Moroccan dishes, especially for Shabbat and yom tov [holiday] meals, one baby step at a time. At least once a year either my mother-in-law or sister-in-law would visit—not those four-day American-style visits, but four-*week* or two-month Moroccan visits! After all, as far as they were concerned, it didn't pay to come all the way from overseas for just a brief stay. Unlike the

Italian opinion that guests, like fish, start to stink after three days, the Moroccan philosophy is the more the merrier.

During those visits my female relatives would take over my kitchen, thereby assuring that their husbands would get all the Moroccan dishes they were so attached to (instead of having to suffer through my inexpert, American-style meals). I stayed on the sidelines as sous-chef, peeling vegetables and washing pots and observing everything they did. There were no recipes—my mother-in-law made it clear she thought recipes were for wimps and amateurs—only ingredients and a rough sense of proportions. After each visit they made, I incorporated a few new dishes into my repertoire. Given that my husband had left his milieu and family to come to America with me, I felt the least I could do to help his general sense of deracination was to cook all the foods he was used to.

As I slowly perfected my culinary techniques, I realized that skill in the kitchen, like marriage, does not spring to life fully formed; it requires trial and error, a few mistakes, the occasional tears, and a few well-chosen expletives from time to time. Cooking *evolves* over the years, becoming (like marriage, one hopes) easier, smoother, and less prone to both minor screwups and full-fledged disasters. You experiment: you learn just how long to let things stew, you learn when the circumstances call for gentle molding or vigorous beating (not your *spouse*, of course), you learn when to try some new technique and when the old standards are what's in order. And in the end, the goal is to achieve, as in marriage, a harmonious union of tastes that can excite and nourish both body and soul.

Reaching Critical Mass

I originally learned to cook Moroccan style to please my husband, but before I knew it my husband and I weren't the only folks around whose palates I had to please. Pretty soon there was a small crowd of hungry children around, children who grew up on Moroccan food but also learned, once they got into school, all the American options like pizza and macaroni-and-cheese and hamburgers (thank you, yeshivas, for teaching my children the disgusting practice of dousing everything from rice to macaroni to eggs in ketchup). I bought some of those Boro Park-size pots; I found shortcuts; since baby brain left me with no concentration for serious reading, I read cooking magazines. Anyway, I was always hungry—during the decade I spent mostly pregnant or nursing, I found myself intrigued by all sorts of odd recipes I never would have looked at twice had I not been in the throes of violent hormone swings. The years I spent home with my kids gave me time to spend hours playing around in the kitchen, dabbling in offbeat recipes and concocting inventive ways to disguise leftovers.

As the kids got older and some of them became teenagers, they really started to *eat!*—more than *me!*—and cooking family meals became serious business! The Shabbat food that used to last from Friday night to Tuesday was suddenly gone by Sunday afternoon and sometimes even Saturday night. I lost my motivation to do complicated baking, because I would put in three hours making a strawberry custard galette or chocolate mousse-and-meringue torte and it would be gone before you could say *Shabbat shalom*. I started looking for recipes that yielded larger quantities and required fewer steps.

When the kids were little, I could invite four guests for Shabbat and count on needing only six or eight full-sized portions; then everybody got bigger, and we were eight full-sized portions all by our lonesomes. We bought a bigger dining room table. We outgrew our six-quart electric crock pot. I went back to Boro Park and bought a few more of those industrial-sized stockpots. I even had to learn tricks like labeling frozen cookies "Raw Gefilte Fish" to make sure they wouldn't disappear before Shabbat had a chance to arrive.

Children are a natural vehicle to help parents to integrate into a community, as we make friends at PTA meetings and the bus stop. As our kids grew, they became friendly with other Jewish kids from every imaginable background. My husband joined a synagogue whose congregation was comprised of the odd combination of North Africans, Israelis, and Syrian Jews from not only Syria but Argentina, Mexico, and Venezuela. As we went to bar mitzvahs and weddings and ate in different sorts of homes, I absorbed, quite literally, rather a lot of different types of Sephardic cooking (some of which is still clinging obstinately to my waistline).

Food is a wonderful gateway for learning about other cultures. As you enter other people's kitchens, and eat at their parties, you engage in a dialogue about their style of living, their priorities, their perspectives. Personally, I found it amusing to witness the rivalries that exist even between the Sephardim themselves; every group believes, quite chauvinistically, that *they* are the most cultured and high-class, and *their* food is the most gourmet and delectable.

The following humble cookbook is the result of many years of mingling with all sorts of Sephardic Jews, while living in mostly Ashkenazic Orthodox Brooklyn. Today gourmet chefs boast of "fusion" cuisine, as they put together unlikely combinations like Thai-Cuban. But my cooking is also fusion cuisine—when I cook for a holiday, every Jewish culture is fair game. I think my life has been wonderfully enriched by living in the center of a cultural crossroads, and so has my cooking. I present you this book—snapshots of my life and my kitchen—in the hopes that it will enrich your life and your cuisine as well.

Part One

The Heavenly Tastes of Shabbat

Introduction: Keeping Shabbat Special

Despite all the effort, and being either an idiot or a hopelessly stubborn purist (or both), I always insist on making everything homemade for Shabbat and the holidays. Not for me takeout chickens, spongy bakery challahs, drippy plastic containers of cole slaw and cucumber salad. (It has always mystified me to see people buying takeout cucumber salad: How hard is it to slice a cucumber?) I'll settle for the occasional takeout pizza or chicken special for a weekday emergency, but takeout for *Shabbat*?! Heresy! My friends told me I was crazy. My guests begged for more.

As much as I know that "modern" women take shortcuts, that the housewife of the twenty-first century has better things to do than spend hours in the kitchen, I am very old-fashioned on this point. I didn't grow up with Shabbat, and now that I have regained it, I refuse to take it for granted. Perhaps I'm overcompensating, but I am really ready, week after week, to pull out all the stops for Shabbat, whether we have guests to impress or not.

There is another reason that I feel so strongly about

throwing myself wholeheartedly into Shabbat preparations, and that is what in Hebrew is called *chinuch*: teaching one's children the Jewish way. Children absorb less what we say than what we *do*, and I want my kids to grow up seeing that Mommy thinks Shabbat is worth spending more than one or two begrudged hours preparing for. In my Brooklyn neighborhood today it is quite possible to buy all one's Shabbat food at the caterer's, and many people avail themselves of this convenience with alacrity. I understand that some women can't abide the kitchen, and that others are working and are simply at a loss for time, but I want my kids to feel that Shabbat is something our family *invested* ourselves into, that we helped *create*; there just isn't the same excitement for a kid to come home and find a bag of bakery challah on the dining room table as there is to come home to a house filled with the aroma of challah puffing up golden and crusty in the oven. I'll never forget the spring afternoon one of my kids came running in from school panting excitedly, "Mommy, Mommy! You left the windows open and we could smell your challah all the way down the block!" In its childish spontaneity, it was one of the sweetest compliments I'd ever received.

All those tastes and smells unique to Shabbat make it an experience that literally gets under one's skin. We joke about good food being a spiritual experience, but it's not so far from the truth; in Judaism, the physical and spiritual are interwoven, as we seek to elevate the material world by investing it with holiness. That's one reason every holiday is marked by its own special foods: matzoh at Pesach, hamantaschen on Purim, blintzes for Shavuoth.

So even if our children don't absorb all the subtle spiritual nuances of Shabbat, they will always remember it for its special meals. And in today's world of gourmet restaurants, of sushi bars and Thai cuisine and corner bistros, you don't want your

Shabbat and holiday food to seem plain and poor in comparison. What a humiliation for Shabbat if the table we set is many steps below the delicacies we have accustomed ourselves to eat on weeknights, if we set out jarred gefilte fish and boiled chicken after a week of eating angel hair pasta and kosher dim sum! How could you possibly entice a non-religious Jew to give up Friday nights at the bistro if Shabbat food is unappealing and tasteless?

Don't get me wrong: Shabbat is much more than a culinary experience. It includes the spiritual joys of prayer and learning Torah, the emotional fulfillment of spending time with one's family, and more down-to-earth pleasures like catching a nap or getting lost in a good book. But the special meals give structure to the day, and impose relaxed times where family members can enjoy unhurried conversations and the children can relate what happened in school that week. People pray in the synagogue, but it's at the Shabbat table that the little ones bring out question sheets from their teachers, the older ones elaborate on the weekly Torah portion, and Jewish topics are discussed. We may all go our separate ways later, but everybody has to eat, and as our meals unify us for food they strengthen our unity as a family on other levels as well.

In this age of computers and iPods and cell phones, not to mention takeout dinners and overloaded schedules, our besieged family lives are fairly crying out for rescue by a weekly Sabbath. Why not cook some satisfying, homemade food, turn off all the machines and gadgets, and enjoy a relaxing, reinvigorating day of family time and spiritual connection? Because the old Shabbat maxim is true: if we invest ourselves in Shabbat, and make the effort to keep it with joy and enthusiasm, it will keep our families and ourselves more happy, more whole, and more Jewish.

Chapter 1

Challah and Other Heavenly Delights

W‍HEN I WAS a kid in public elementary school, the straws for our little milk cartons came in a paper wrapper printed with blue letters reading "BREAD IS THE STAFF OF LIFE." This always puzzled me. Maybe they meant the "stuff" of life? Maybe people used those long French baguettes as a cane? Only later did I realize they were trying to say that bread supports life, that it is in fact so central to diets everywhere that to "earn one's daily bread" stands for supplying all of one's needs.

Bread defines a meal in Torah culture. A meal has the status of a *seudah* (formal meal) if the participants ritually wash their hands and bless the bread at its beginning. Only if we eat bread do we recite the lengthy *birkat hamazon* blessing in thanks at the end of a meal. It is a sad sign of the times that kosher bakers have recently come up with a product known as "*mezonos* bread," i.e., bread that technically has the status of cake and does not require *hamotzi* or *birkat hamazon*, knowing that many Jews today lack the time (or, more to the point, the patience) for long after-blessings. Perhaps we also have a harder time summoning up the proper attitude of gratitude for our food; nowadays, for what is surely the first time in history, we fret considerably more about *over*-consuming it than we do about finding enough to eat.

Many of my friends who grew up in Morocco recall that their mothers made bread every single day. Perhaps the maid helped with the kneading, and she certainly helped with the cleanup, but those Jewish mothers took it for granted that part of their daily routine involved baking fresh bread for their families. I have tasted Moroccan bread, and found it tasty and wholesome, made with whole wheat flour and sprinkled with anise and sesame. My mother-in-law also used to make a slightly sweet, brioche-style bread called *mona* as an after-school treat.

But today bread baking has become a lost art in most circles. Most women simply aren't *home* enough to make *home*-made bread, which requires being around every couple of hours to punch down the dough and keep an eye on it in the oven. Others give it a try once or twice, and if they don't get bakery-perfect results, throw up their hands in defeat and never try again. Bread-baking is not mastered as easily as making cake or cookies, and ideally requires an afternoon of apprenticeship with someone who knows what she's doing.

The actual ingredients of bread are laughably simple: flour, yeast, water, salt; the precise quantities are less important than the way the dough looks and feels before it goes in to rise. *That's* what you really need to learn to produce good bread, and you can't get it from just reading a recipe. But the artisanal character and lack of precision are exactly what makes baking bread so satisfying. Making a cake is a structured, cut-and-dried affair, where you have to measure meticulously and not deviate too much from the instructions. Bread, however, is more organic; it's never the same each time you make it, depending on the weather and the flour and all sorts of other mysterious factors (for example, according to Moroccan old wives' tales, the challah will flop if a husband and wife are not getting along). Some days the dough comes together in a stiff dry ball and you have to keep adding water; sometimes it's too sticky, so you're continually adding flour. The weather will affect it too-- when hot the dough will rise quickly, sometimes practically climbing out of the bowl, while cold weather makes it sluggish.

New Yorkers all have their own stories to tell about the Blackout of 2003, and mine involves challah. A newlywed friend of mine had come over that Thursday afternoon to take a lesson in making Moroccan salads. My challahs, already shaped, was sitting in aluminum pans on the kitchen table, covered with a towel, and we were chatting about this and that when the light suddenly went out. Then I noticed that the numbers on the microwave had disappeared. "A fuse must have blown," we said. My friend started to go home to find her husband, who's handy with electricity. But she came back a few seconds later with a funny look on her face. "I think it's the whole neighborhood," she said. "Look, the traffic light on the corner is out." And sure enough, there were Brooklyn drivers inching through the intersection, suddenly, shockingly polite ("After you." "No, after you...").

Anyway, I have a gas oven with an electric ignition, and we had no idea how to ignite it manually. I went all up and down my block looking for somebody with an old-fashioned gas oven with a pilot light, but nobody had one. So my poor challahs rose and rose and rose and rose until they just couldn't keeping stretching any more. I could almost hear them crying "Oof!" as they collapsed down into doughy heaps in their pans. I was very sad when I finally dumped them into the garbage, but fortunately Boro Park had electricity by 4:00 a.m. and we were able to buy bakery challah trucked in the next morning. (We ourselves didn't get power until an hour before Shabbat, but you could hear whoops of joy and relief all up and down the block as people ran to turn on their air conditioners and lights before candle-lighting time. We should only wait for the Messiah with the same impatience!)

The Spiritual Side of Challah Baking

There are those who turn challah baking into a whole devotional exercise. I once read an article in a Jewish magazine addressed to the famous (or infamous) Dr. Laura Schlesinger, a radio personality who became an enthusiastic convert to Judaism and then announced she was pulling back because she no longer found the same level of inspiration in it. Well, this writer decided to show Dr. Laura that "inspiration" is what you make of it, and that spirituality begins at home. To prove her point, she chose to demonstrate what a spiritual experience challah baking is in the inner sanctum of her kitchen. She elaborated at length about the way she and her daughter take turns kneading the dough, always with utmost *kavanah* (spiritual intention). Then they lift it up with both hands, crying "*Zot ha-challah!*"—this is the challah!-- before separating a piece to burn as *terumah*. (In the days of the Temple, women separated a portion of their bread dough, called *terumah*, to donate to the priests. Today, in the absence of the Temple, we still separate a piece of dough to preserve the tradition for the day when it will, G-d willing, be rebuilt. This is more than a nostalgic tradition, by the way; it's a *halacha* serious enough so that one is not permitted to eat bread from which *terumah* was not taken properly.)

Now I have to admit this woman rather put me to shame, for my own weekly challah-baking is a more prosaic, routine affair than a lofty spiritual experience. But then again, perhaps she's on to something. Nowadays foodies worship good food, but they've really got it backwards: *food* is meant as a vehicle for *worship*; in Judaism, it's through the most everyday physical acts that a Jew strives to connect to the Divine.

One charming story which illustrates this point tells of a Chasid who sat at his rebbe's *tisch* (table), while both of them were eating apples. "Rebbe," the Chasid asked, "I make a *bracha* [blessing] and eat my apple, you also make a *bracha* and eat your apple. So what is the difference between the two of us?" The Rebbe answered dryly: "The difference is that *you* make a *bracha* in order to eat the apple, but *I* eat the apple in order to make a *bracha!*"

Most of us aren't on the level of this Rebbe; we make *hamotzi* eagerly anticipating that first mouthful of bread, and the pleasure is magnified immeasurably when the bread came from your own oven. As one of our guests once remarked perceptively: "When the challah comes from the bakery, it's just regular, plain old challah. But when it's homemade, making the blessing and cutting the bread become an *event.*" The whole table sits in breathless expectation of that first slice, wondering how delicious it will be this week.

In fact, that's the problem once you have mastered bread technique and start producing truly mouth-watering challah: your family will never let you bring home the store-bought kind again. Then you will find yourself saddled with the responsibility of baking bread every week or two.

But then again, why not? If you think about it, aren't our families—and isn't Shabbat—worth our best efforts? A working woman makes more than enough per hour to absorb the extra cost of bakery bread, but the smell of homemade bread filling her home is beyond any dollar value. So is the message to her children that she's eager to go the extra mile to make the family Shabbat something truly special.

11

Basic Challah Recipe

This is my best "Challah for Dummies" recipe. One of the biggest mistakes challah novices make is to work too much flour into the dough, since bread dough feels so sticky on the hands, but the result is a heavy loaf better employed as a doorstop. This recipe kneads the dough in a food processor, so you're less likely to make this mistake. The recipe makes one large challah, but since it goes so quickly, you can simply make one loaf, dump out the dough, and repeat the process as many times as you like. In the interests of sneaking some nutrition into my white-bread-loving children, I usually add a tablespoon of wheat germ to the dough.

2 teaspoons dry yeast (1 package) dissolved in ½ cup very warm water along with ½ teaspoon sugar
3 cups flour, preferably high-gluten
2-3 tablespoons sugar
1 ½ teaspoons salt
1 tablespoon wheat germ (optional)
1 egg
1/3 cup oil
1/3 cup plus a couple tablespoons water
1 beaten egg for glazing the challah; sesame or poppy seeds for garnishing, if desired
Cooking spray and corn meal to grease the pans

Place flour, sugar, salt and wheat germ in the bowl of the food processor and pulse to blend. Add the yeast-and-water mix (it should be foamy after five minutes) and process another 5-10 seconds. Combine an egg and 1/3 cup oil and water into a small bowl; now dump this into the processor and continue processing until the mixture forms a ball around the blades of the machine—this may take 20-30 seconds (if you have a plastic dough knife for your machine, use it; if not, a regular steel blade will also do the trick). Check the dough; if it seems tough and dry, add a couple of tablespoons of water; if it seems too wet and won't come together, add more flour, ¼ cup at a time.

Let the dough process on a medium-low speed for one minute. Voila! The dough is done. Place into an oiled bowl, turn it once, cover it with a plastic bag, and let it rise until doubled, about an hour and a half (it may rise faster if your kitchen is hot).

Punch it down and repeat the rising (it's not absolutely necessary to do two risings, but I think it makes a smoother loaf). The second rising may go faster than the first. When doubled again, punch down the dough. Shape into a loaf, either by braiding it or, as my mother-in-law does, by rolling it into a long rectangle from which you cut a fringe on one end and roll it up. (I only recently mastered braiding with six strands, but an easier, and also very nice, option is to divide the dough into four parts. Braid three of them, then make a skinny braid with the fourth part. Slice a little trough down the length of the big braid with a knife and nestle the smaller braid inside it—this will keep it from sliding off during baking, and makes a pretty double-braided shape.) I like to use aluminum loaf pans to bake my challahs, as the high sides help them rise and maintain a more professional, uniform shape; spray them with cooking spray and dust with corn meal.

Preheat oven to 425 degrees. Let your shaped challahs rise at least another half hour, until almost doubled in size. Brush with the beaten egg and top with seeds if desired (I like to get creative making patterns with white and black sesame seeds). Bake at 425 for ten minutes, then reduce oven temperature to 375 and bake until golden brown, about another half hour. For a crispier crust, take the challahs out of the pans (carefully!) for the last five minutes of baking. When they're done, the bottoms will sound hollow when tapped with your finger.

Variation: Whole Wheat Challah

My husband decided he prefers whole wheat or whole spelt challahs, as they're more nutritious and he finds them easier on the digestion. It's advisable to mix whole wheat flour with regular bread flour, as the whole grain flour contains much less gluten and consequently will not rise very well all by itself. You can simply use the recipe above, but substitute about two-thirds of the white flour with whole wheat or whole spelt flour.

A Note on Sephardic Shaping

When my mother-in-law visits us, she makes her challah in a shape I had never seen before. Instead of braiding the dough, she manages to create a sort of striped loaf. I soon saw how this was accomplished; she rolls out the dough into a long rectangle. Then she cuts one of the narrow ends into a sort of long fringe. Starting from the opposite end, she rolls the dough rectangle into a loaf, ending with the "fringes" wrapped around the loaf decoratively. When baked, the fringes puff into a striped pattern.

My husband was familiar with this Moroccan challah shape and immediately surmised that it must have some ancient mystical significance; perhaps there was even a specified number of stripes to cut, like those who have the custom to bake a dozen challah rolls for every Shabbat. But when he asked his mother the reason behind this unusual shape, she merely shrugged. "Who knows?" she said. "I think it's just a way of making the challah easier to slice." And indeed, when you bring the striped challahs to the table, the indentations between the stripes make perfect cutting guides!

Petits Pains aux Chocolat

Every time my mother-in-law visits she leaves us with a new favorite, and this one is wicked good straight from the oven. It's a sweet bread dough baked with a square of melted chocolate inside. Most bakery petits pains aux chocolat *use a puff pastry dough, but this dough is very soft and fragrant. I usually put up a batch when I finish making my challah dough—no need to wash out the machine in between!*

I used to bake a bunch of these every week as a special Shabbat breakfast for the kids—but I always had to double the recipe, since everybody pounced on them as soon as they came out of the oven, and there were bitter fights if somebody took more than his share!

1 packet (2 ¼ teaspoons) yeast and 1 teaspoon sugar dissolved in scant ½ cup very warm water
3 cups flour
1/3 cup sugar
½ teaspoon salt
Grated zest of an orange or lemon
5 tablespoons margarine
1 egg
1/3 cup orange juice
1 teaspoon vanilla
1 beaten egg and extra sugar for glazing
1 fine-quality semi-sweet or bittersweet chocolate bar

Place flour, sugar, salt and zest in the bowl of the food processor and pulse to blend. Add margarine, cut in chunks, and process about 10 seconds. Add yeast mixture (should be foamy) and blend. Combine the egg, orange juice and vanilla in a small bowl and dump into the processor as well, and process until mixture forms a ball on the blades (this will make a slightly softer dough than the challah dough). Process another 30-45 seconds.

Let rise, covered with a plastic bag, in an oiled bowl. Sweet doughs take longer to rise than regular doughs, so give it a good two to two and a half hours to rise. Punch down and, if you have the time, let it rise again.

Divide the dough into about fifteen balls. Roll each ball out into a rectangle, about four inches by six inches. Put a square of dark chocolate at one end of the rectangle (I break it in half and lay the halves end to end). Roll in the sides slightly and roll up the whole thing stuffed-cabbage style. Repeat with each ball and lay rolls seam-side down on a greased baking sheet. Let rise until puffy and almost doubled.

Brush rolls with beaten egg and a sprinkling of sugar. Bake at 350 degrees for about twenty minutes, until golden. Best eaten while the chocolate inside is still melty!

Afterward: Saving Your Bread

Bread merits so much respect in Jewish tradition that one is not supposed to waste it (a sentiment that is only amplified when you have spent the better part of an afternoon kneading, checking, and baking it). It should never be cavalierly tossed into the garbage, with the exception of crumbs or crusts too small or hard to eat. Ideally, bread that is no longer wanted should be given to animals to eat or recycled in some way, shape or form. Over the years I have come up with various useful ways to recycle bread, most of which are easy enough to do:

1. French toast—soaking slices of bread in beaten egg, then frying them and serving with maple syrup, honey, jam or confectioner's sugar.

2. Homemade bread crumbs: trim slices of bread of hard crusts, lay on a baking sheet and dry them out in a 250-degree oven for a couple of hours (this will insure that they'll keep for a long time instead of sprouting icky green mold). Then whirl them in a food processor to make crumbs.

3. Homemade croutons: Same idea, but cut your bread slices into cubes before drying them in the oven. To make flavored cubes, I spray the cubes lightly with cooking spray before I bake them and sprinkle with salt, garlic powder, dried parsley and oregano or thyme.

4. Bread pudding: my friend Yael once brought a Pyrex dish full of it as a dessert for a meal in our succah. It's on the heavy and filling side as desserts go, but on a cold winter night it is the apex of comfort food, warm and sweet and definitely not diminished by the addition of a nice melty scoop of vanilla ice cream on top.

5. Garlic bread: spread a generous layer of butter, margarine or olive oil on the bread, sprinkle with garlic powder, kosher salt, and if you like some za'atar or dried parsley, and put under the broiler for a couple of minutes.

6. Similar to this but more trendy is bruschetta, where you brush the bread with olive oil and top with a mixture of chopped tomatoes, onions and basil before broiling.

And if everybody really, really doesn't want to help use up

the bread—for example the teenage girls decided to go on a low-carb diet and the boys balk at having to wash and say *birkat hamazon*—then for heaven's sake crumble it into a pan and put it outside for the neighborhood birds, who I can assure you will not quibble over carbs or *brachas* and will be happy to entertain your younger children by feeding happily on your Shabbat leftovers.

Chapter 2

Salad Days: La Tchouktchouka

AMERICANS, particularly girls and women on perpetual diets, are very attached to their "salads," which these days seems to mean a bag of prewashed lettuce doused with bottled dressing. For picnics and barbecues, "salad" means starchy vegetables lavishly creamed with mayonnaise, like potato salad or macaroni salad. And when you order a salad in a tony restaurant, there the all-but-politically-incorrect iceberg lettuce has been replaced by more exotic varieties with names like *arugula* and *radicchio*, dressed with high-end ingredients like cold-pressed extra-extra virgin olive oil and balsamic vinegar produced by chanting monks high in the Tuscan hills.

But "salad" has a much broader meaning when it comes to Sephardic, and particularly Moroccan, food. In the same way that the Ashkenazi cook will mix almost any vegetable with eggs and flour, bake it and call it a "kugel," for Moroccans almost any vegetable is fair game to be chopped up and/or cooked, dressed and called a salad. A Moroccan salad could be anything from beets squirted with lemon and pressed garlic to peppers grilled and sliced to sweet oranges mixed with the unlikely but tasty combination of black olives and hot paprika. In fact, the one salad you will not see on a Moroccan table is lettuce leaves—heavens, that would be too *easy*!

Having married my Nice Jewish Boy from Casablanca, once we set up housekeeping I found myself entering a new style of entertaining that included making a large variety of Moroccan salads every week for Shabbos...er, *Shabbat*. This takes up more time than just about everything else I do for Shabbat, and today a lot of Sephardic women can't be bothered to make more than one or two on their own. Maybe *Ima* or *Maman* made all that stuff every week, they'll tell you, but hey, back in Morocco she had maids, and what else was there to do back there anyway?

Today we don't have the cheap maids or the slower-paced life; what we have are prepackaged kosher salads available at the grocery store in little plastic tubs for those who feel life is too short or too busy to spend slaving away in a hot kitchen. (There's a new trend to buy "dips," which too often are little more than cooked vegetables drowning in mayonnaise.) But store-bought is never, ever as good or as fresh as homemade, and if you're home anyway due to young children or unemployment or waiting for the plumber to show up, I can think of few more constructive ways to pass the time than cook up a few delicious Moroccan salads.

Starting a meal with a large variety of vegetables is a nutritionist's dream. Contrary to popular myth, Moroccan salads do not have to be drenched in oil, and in many cases olive oil is used. The idea is to pass around the salad bowls so that everybody gets to sample a little bit of everything, which at a well-appointed table guarantees the ingestion of just about every major vitamin. The amount of garlic, raw and cooked, that one can ingest after filling one's plate with Moroccan salads is probably enough to preclude the need for any blood-thinning medications for at least a month or two. Just one warning: no matter how many and varied the salads are on your Shabbat or yom tov table, you will never, ever be able to win the Most Moroccan Salads contest. If your guests are Moroccan, then some lady is sure to say with a sniff as she surveys your table, "Oh my, you made *ten* salads? You went to so much trouble! Of course, *I* always make at least fifteen—that's when we *don't* have guests of course..."

Moroccan salads could merit an entire cookbook on their own, but let's begin with a quintessential Moroccan staple. This is a salad with the percussive name of *tchouktchouka*, and in the same way Anita Bryant used to say that breakfast without orange juice is like a day without sunshine, you might fairly say that for Moroccans Shabbat without *tchouktchouka* is like Chanukah without doughnuts.

Tchouktchouka is a cooked salad of bell peppers, tomatoes, garlic and spices, simmered for hours until the vegetables have cooked down and the whole thing has acquired the consistency of chutney. You slather it on challah or simply eat it by the fork-ful. Those familiar with "Israeli" salads will know this salad as *matbucha*, which is what they call it over there. But I have never heard Moroccans who were born and raised in Morocco call it anything but *tchouktchouka*, which is certainly a much cuter name—it brings to mind steam locomotives, or some new South American dance rhythm ("Can you do the *tchouk-tchouka?*").

I have never met anybody who didn't like tchouktchouka, not even the most dyed-in-the-wool, matzoh-ball-fed Ashkenazim. It is a real staple of the Moroccan Shabbat table, and I have passed on the tchouktchouka *mesorah* [tradition] to more than a few guests who, despite the fact that it is time-consuming (a *potchke*, in good Yiddish) have made it a standard part of their Shabbat repertoire (now proudly holding its place of honor right next to the gefilte fish and potato kugel). To give you an idea of tchouktchouka's broad appeal, my friend Debbie, who took down my recipe fifteen years ago and still makes it every week, has moved around all over the East Coast and in every location has spread the tradition to an ever-increasing circle of devotees. My friend Yael, who married a Klausenberger Chasid and subsequently undertook seamed stockings, hat-topped wigs and the Yiddish language, makes tchouktchouka every week for her Chasidic family, and is often persuaded to give some away to her eager Borough Park neighbors as well.

The joy of tchouktchouka is that not only is it very tasty, it is a gift that keeps on giving: once Shabbat is over it miraculously transforms into a condiment with fabulous, unlimited possibilities, some of which I will be happy to give over at the end of this chapter.

My family likes their tchouktchouka cooked right up to the point where the whole thing is just on the point of burning (the Moroccans called this "caramelized"). This will keep your kitchen warm for a few hours in the winter (it will also occupy one of the burners of your stove for as long), but I must admit on a hot August afternoon only habit and gluttony compel me to persist in the folly of making a salad that requires two hours of simmer time. (In fact, as far as I am concerned it is one of the Great Unsolved Mysteries of the World why, in a country with a climate as scorchingly hot as Morocco's, just about everything they cook requires hours upon hours of stewing on a hot stove: What were they *thinking?*)

Tchouktchouka definitely requires some effort; the peppers have to be charred, peeled and diced, the garlic peeled and chopped, the tomatoes torn or cut into chunks. In Morocco, where my sister-in-law still lives, for some reason they can't get canned whole peeled tomatoes, which is what I always use. But rather than forego tchouktchouka, she and her maids spend every Wednesday afternoon scalding fresh tomatoes and peeling them, just in order to be able to make tchouktchouka on Thursday for the Shabbat table Friday night. (I imagine the tchouktchouka has an even fresher taste made this way, but even *I* have to admit life's too short to undertake this sort of labor unless you absolutely have no choice.) It consequently takes my sister-in-law and her household help several hours of joint effort to produce a few modest bowls of tchouktchouka, a quantity her teenage son could easily polish off single-handedly and often does (said son, who is otherwise a nice enough boy, once devoured in my house the major part of a bowl of tchouktchouka meant to last through a three-day *yom tov*, as I sat at the other end of the table watching in horror. After that I got smart and started rationing it out over *yom tov* meals).

There are only two drawbacks to tchouktchouka. The first is that the stuff is addictive, and once you get hooked on it there's no turning back. You will find yourself spending every erev Shabbat with the smell of charring peppers and stewing tomatoes filling your house and making all the neighbors jealous. The second drawback is that it tends to end up as orange stains on the cuffs of little boys' Shabbat shirts. That of course only raises the question, whose idea was it to dress little boys in white shirts for Shabbat anyway? ---wouldn't dark colors have been so much more practical, at least for those under bar mitzvah age? But this is not a problem in short sleeve weather, unless your kids are also masters of dripping food down the front of their shirts as well.

But enough said; let me tell you how to make the stuff already.

Tchouktchouka

2 red bell peppers
2 green bell peppers
½ a jalapeno pepper, chopped, or ½ teaspoon red pepper
flakes (totally optional)
5-6 cloves garlic, coarsely chopped
2 tbsp cooking oil
2 tsp sweet paprika
salt to taste (optional; there's already salt in canned tomatoes,
and I usually omit it myself)
3 28-oz cans peeled whole tomatoes (you can substitute diced
tomatoes)

Char the peppers under the broiler, turning every few minutes, until blackened on all sides; place in a plastic bag to cool. The blackened exterior should slip off easily when cooled. Wash peppers well, removing seeds, and cut into dice.

Throw the diced peppers into a nice heavy-bottomed saucepan with the oil, garlic, jalapeno and spices. Let this simmer over medium heat while you open your cans of tomatoes and begin tearing the tomatoes into small chunks and adding them to the pan. Once the entire mixture is simmering, reduce heat to low and let it continue to cook, stirring occasionally, for at least two hours, until the liquid has evaporated and the mixture has darkened in color and looks like preserves. Serve at room temperature with thick slices of challah.

Now that you have your tchouktchouka, and Shabbat is over, what do you do with the leftovers? There are enough tasty options to ensure you will never have to throw it in the garbage.

Tchouktchouka is much tastier and classier than ketchup as a condiment in sandwiches, including hot sandwiches like hamburgers or franks. It makes a terrific filling for omelettes. It can be added to thicken and flavor plain tomato sauce or thinned with olive oil and used as a pasta sauce. Try adding half a cup of tchouktchouka to a few cups of leftover rice, with a can of tomato sauce and a little cayenne or hot paprika; bake this in a 350-degree oven for half an hour and you will have a very nice platter of Spanish rice.

My personal favorite when it comes to using up the tchouk-tchouka is to put it in homemade pizza. It makes a great substitute for tomato sauce. Since the only oven I have large enough to accommodate a full-size pizza is reserved for meat dishes, and my husband's a bit lactose-intolerant, I generally make cheeseless pizza. I spread 1 ½ to 2 cups of tchouktchouka over the pizza dough (you can use homemade or purchased dough), then sprinkle a couple of cans of crumbled tuna on top. This then gets topped with a couple of sautéed onions and, when the mood hits, sliced olives and/or anchovies and/or fried slices of eggplant. Spinach and broccoli are also very good toppings; you can pre-saute them right along with the onions. I once bought a pizza pan in a restaurant-supply store that was designed with small holes all over the bottom, and it turns out pizza with a thin crispy crust that rivals anything the gourmet brick-oven pizza places can produce.

Now I challenge all of you to find even more creative ways to recycle the tchouktchouka. If you have any left, that is. It may take two hours to cook, but—especially if your Shabbat table tends to accommodate a small crowd—it has a way of disappearing faster than you can say *Shabbat Shalom*!

Chapter 3

Appetizing Appetizers: Olives and Eggplant a la Fatima

ONE SUMMER, shortly after our sixth child was born, my sister-in-law in Marrakech decided to send me two of her kids for the summer. In their tiny community in Morocco, there isn't much for Jewish kids to do during the torrid summers; in Brooklyn they could at least go to day camp and sightsee in Manhattan. Since I had six kids myself, and the oldest was only nine, my sister-in-law had the bright idea to send along an Arab maid to ease the extra burden it would impose. (Said sister-in-law, who has at least two live-in maids for a family of five, could never understand how I managed to get by with twice as many children and not even one live-in).

Fatima, our new maid, arrived with our niece and nephew looking shell-shocked from her first plane ride and smelling faintly of the farm. But she quickly recovered and set about attacking my house. Her idea of cleaning a room, I soon found out, was to empty it of all of its furniture (massive bookcases included), remove the entire rug and wash the floor underneath, and rearrange all our furniture and throw out our old clothing whether we liked it or not.

Life with Fatima was like living with Dr. Jekyll and Mr. Hyde. One day we were the best of friends, sharing jokes and a pot of mint tea and Moroccan pastries, and the next day she could wake up in a murderous mood looking like she was itching to pour a bowl of boiling oil on top of us (which, she told us, was the latest fashion for disgruntled Moroccan wives who wished to dispatch their husbands quickly and painfully). We tried terribly hard to make Fatima happy, paying her well above what she would have gotten back home, buying her tapes of her favorite Arab singers (not to mention putting up with hearing them nonstop), treating her with exaggerated respect. But, sadly, as is so often the case in Jewish –Arab relations, our hopes that our kind and fair treatment would be reciprocated with gratitude and mutual respect simply backfired on us. Fatima interpreted our softness not as benevolence but as lack of backbone and an opportunity to push the limits, and no matter how much time and money we consecrated to her she always managed to find a reason to flare up in a rage against us.

But aside from the education she provided me with in the Mahgrebian personality in microcosm, Fatima also imparted some of her considerable culinary knowledge to me. She knew how to make *shebakia*, a honey-dipped sesame pastry favored by my husband, and *sloe*, a halvah-like concoction that involves baking raw flour in the oven until it turns brown and mixing in a lot of melted margarine, sugar, sesame seeds and nuts (I never even tried reproducing that one, as my husband was the only person who seemed to like it, and the whole house smelled like burned flour the night she made it.)

But there are a couple of Moroccan salads I picked up from Fatima that I still make. The first is a way of preparing olives that even non-olive eaters often like, the reason being that the Moroccans like to boil olives before using them in cooking to take out some of the salt and bitterness. (I usually double this recipe because in my house they disappear very fast.) The second is a fried eggplant salad that is so delicious that I am willing to turn a blind eye to the many excess calories it surely contains and am even willing to invest half an hour standing next to a hot frying pan to make it (although perhaps this is not something I would recommend making on a day there's a heat advisory, or you expect little children to be underfoot a lot!)

In the years since Fatima left, I have made do with part-time cleaning help from cheerful Mexicans who never fume under their breath as they clean, or scream at my children, or oblige us to listen to the wailing of Oum Khartoum. But I must admit that Fatima was a tremendous help at a time when I needed it, and I will try to retain the good things I learned from her even while enjoying the vast relief of knowing her moods and anger are safely back in Morocco!

Moroccan Olives

2 15-ounce cans large pitted green olives
1 cup water
1/3 cup olive oil or salad oil
2 cloves garlic, minced or run through a press
1 teaspoon turmeric (*curcum*)
2 teaspoons za'atar (an Oriental spice comprised of hyssop —optional)
2 tablespoons tomato paste
Dash salt
¼ lemon, sliced
1 tablespoon chopped parsley or cilantro
1 teaspoon red pepper flakes (or to taste)

Open the can of olives, drain them, and put in a pot with water to cover. Bring to a boil, let simmer for several minutes, then drain the water. Add the cup of fresh water and the next seven ingredients; let simmer until the water has evaporated (about twenty minutes). Add parsley and pepper flakes, stir to mix and serve.

Fried Eggplant Salad

1 large eggplant (long and thin is better than short and fat for this recipe)
Salt
Cooking oil
1 red pepper, charred on all sides on the stove, cooled, peeled, and cut into dice
1 clove garlic
Juice of half a lemon
1 tablespoon chopped parsley or cilantro for garnish
Salt, pepper to taste

Cut the eggplant (unpeeled) into thin slices and sprinkle with salt. Let sit for twenty minutes, then dry any excess moisture with paper towels. Heat oil in a saucepan until piping hot, then fry slices golden brown on both sides, adding more oil as necessary. Mix in remaining ingredients gently and serve. Variation: Cut the eggplant into ½-inch cubes and fry.

Chapter 4

Keep It Simple, Stupid

I've always tried to be a good parent and never miss the Orientation and PTA nights at my children's respective yeshivas. This year, as I walked into Orientation Night at my daughters' school, the principal stopped me. She knows me by name by now, thanks to having had my four daughters pass through the cinderblocked halls of this noble institution (a privilege I like to imagine is both hers and mine).

"Mrs. Bensoussan, I've been enjoying your cooking column in the newspaper," she said. "Although I usually don't try the recipes, because those Sephardic recipes seem so *complicated*. Don't they have any recipes that are, well, a little more *simple*?"

Hmm, I thought as I trudged up the concrete stairs to find my daughter's classroom. *Do* Sephardim have anything simple?

The bitter truth is that I have often heard Sephardic women complain that, in comparison with their Ashkenazic sisters, they have a much tougher culinary row to hoe. "They make Shabbat *chick-chok!*" an Israeli friend moaned with undisguised jealousy. "They throw gefilte fish into one pot of boiling water—that's the fish! Then they throw a chicken into another pot of boiling water—soup! Then they throw a chicken in the oven—chicken! A kugel, a cholent and they're finished. Imagine that!"

Definitely easier than making a large array of fresh and cooked salads, meats that are stuffed into vegetables or stewed with fruits or vegetables, exotic rice dishes, etc. Although, in all fairness, I know many, many enterprising and innovative Ashkenazic *balabustas* who willingly fuss in the kitchen for hours and whose repertoire goes way beyond chicken soup and gefilte fish. The roaring success of the many new glossy Jewish cookbooks on offer is testament to the fact that today's American and other English-speaking kosher cooks are more than eager to experiment with new, upscale, and yes, sometimes even complicated recipes.

But the yeshiva principal got the wheels turning in my mind, and I started thinking about something I could offer that is simple to make. After awhile, it finally came to me: boiled vegetable salads.

Sounds pretty uninspiring, right? As a child there was nothing I detested as much as plain boiled vegetables on my plate. All the fresh taste seemed to have leeched out into the cooking water, and what was left was not redeemed by any sort of inspired seasoning. Worse, I found the mushy texture revolting. I didn't care how many starving children in Asia would have happily gobbled down those vegetables; I would have happily mailed them off to them.

But there are a couple of Moroccan salads that are quite tasty despite being made with boiled vegetables. If you've ever eaten an appetizer of mixed salads at a Middle Eastern restaurant, chances are you've already tasted one or more of them. And they really are quite simple to prepare: peel and boil vegetables, cut them into chunks, spice and eat. The trick is not to overboil the vegetables so they avoid becoming soggy and limp, then power-boost their flavor with vibrant spices.

These salads reformed me of my former abhorrence of boiled vegetables. Cooked carrots became appealing when dressed with garlic, lemon juice and hot paprika. Beets, which I never particularly liked, suddenly took on new charm mixed with cumin and parsley. And potato salad, which I always *did* like, takes on a new appeal prepared Sephardic style with olive oil, lemon juice and allspice.

So, in honor of my daughters' elementary school principal and all those readers who might actually try one of my recipes if it seemed easy enough, here are three reasonably simple recipes for cooked salads that also happen to be yummy. Hopefully from now on the phrase "yummy boiled vegetables" will no longer have to be an oxymoron, and these veggies will be enough of a success at your table that your children will not get any urges to pick up the phone to try to FedEx them off to the starving children in Asia.

Moroccan Carrot Salad

1 pound fresh carrots, peeled, the ends cut off, cut in halves
1 ½ tablespoons oil
Juice of 1/2 lemon
1 clove garlic, run through a press
1 teaspoon tomato paste
½ teaspoon paprika
½ teaspoon cumin
½ teaspoon chili powder
¼ teaspoon hot paprika or cayenne (or to taste)
Salt
¼ cup chopped fresh parsley or cilantro

Cook the carrots in a pot of boiling water until tender but not mushy, about fifteen minutes. While carrots are boiling, mix remaining ingredients together in a bowl (or plastic container with a lid if you're planning to store them). When carrots are cooked, drain and cover with cold water to cool. When cool enough to handle, cut into coins and toss with the dressing.

Barba (Beet Salad)

4-5 large beets
1 clove garlic, run through a press
Juice of 1/2 lemon
1 teaspoon cumin
Salt, pepper
¼ cup chopped fresh parsley or cilantro

Boil the beets, unpeeled, in a pot of water until tender, about 45 minutes to an hour (I often use a pressure cooker to save time; the beets need about fifteen minutes in a pressure cooker. I leave them unpeeled on the assumption that this way they will leach less vitamins into the water while cooking, and because, like potatoes, beets are easier to peel once cooked). Let the boiled beets cool in cold water. Peel them and cut into small chunks. Put them into a bowl or container, add the remaining ingredients, and mix well.

Note 1: Since I first started making Moroccan salads, pre-cooked, pre-peeled, and often organic beets have come onto the market. I buy them often now to save time!
Note 2: Some people buy knives with zigzag blades that cut their carrots and beets into pieces with attractive wavy edges.

Syrian Potato Salad

6-8 large potatoes, unpeeled
3 scallions, chopped
2 hard-boiled eggs, chopped
¼ cup olive oil
Juice of a lemon
Salt, pepper
¼ teaspoon allspice (optional)
Chopped fresh or dried parsley for garnish

Boiled potatoes under tender, about 15-20 minutes. Cool, peel and slice into a bowl or container. Add scallions and eggs. Whisk together remaining ingredients except parsley in a small bowl and pour over potato mixture; stir gently. Garnish with chopped parsley.

Chapter 5

Fish For Compliments

Full of Gefilte

ONE PESACH WEEK, when our children were little, we treated them to an outing at the New York Aquarium. First we wandered through hall after hall of aquariums, including the spooky blue-lit room with the huge tank full of sharks, gliding by menacingly just the other side of the glass. Then we went to watch the trained dolphins and seals cavort in an enormous pool, the kids oohing and aahing at their tricks and squealing as sprays of water flew into the bleachers.

As soon as we got home all the kids tumbled through the door, bursting to tell their grandparents about their exciting day. My father listened with amusement. "Hey," he asked them with a twinkle in his eye, "did you guys get to see the gefilte fish?"

They stopped short, confused. Now which fish had been the gefilte fish?

My mother laughed. "Oh yes," she said, playing along.

"He's the one swimming around with a carrot on top of his head!"

Now you may or may not find this amusing, but my Moroccan husband was no less confused the first time he found himself face to face with actual gefilte fish. "What kind of fish is *sweet?*" he hissed under his breath at my friend's Shabbos table. It didn't even seem like fish---no bones, no skin, and only watery crimson horseradish for a sauce instead of the bright red, garlic- and hot pepper-infused *chermoula* sauce he was used to. "Not everybody makes it sweet," I hissed back. But gefilte fish is strictly a European phenomenon, and where he comes from, this way of cooking fish seemed about as odd as eating oatmeal-stuffed tripe or chocolate covered ants.

All the sources I have read claim that gefilte fish originated as a way to avoid separating the flesh of the fish from the bones on Shabbos. The fish was de-boned and prepared by mashing it together with spices, eggs, onions, carrots and bread crumbs (surely a way to stretch an expensive commodity as well as prolong its freshness in times of limited refrigeration). The word "gefilte" means stuffed, and sometimes people would take the flesh from the fish, chop it up, and re-stuff it into the skin. I saw culinary echoes of this recently at an elegant catered *Shabbos* meal where we were served slices of whitefish that had been stuffed with a gefilte fish mixture and poached in fish broth.

Carp was originally brought to Europe by traders from the Orient, and was quickly adopted by the Jews. A particularly bony fish, it was a logical candidate to be deboned and formed into patties. Today many old-timers remember bringing home a live carp from the fish man in Williamsburg or the Lower East Side and keeping him like a pet in the bathtub until he would tragically meet his doom right before *yom tov.* My personal first encounter with whole, live carp came the first year I lived in

Boro Park. I went out to buy fish for Rosh Hashanah, and walked in to witness the fish man clubbing a gigantic carp to death right before my eyes. The miserable creature refused to die for a torturously long time, thrashing about wildly on the counter—as for me, in the early stages of expecting my first child, I nearly passed out right then and there on the scale-spattered tile floor.

Today, however, most gefilte fish is not made of carp, but rather a combination of other freshwater fishes such a mullet, pike and whitefish. There are those who claim that you can trace an Ashkenazi Jew's origins by two revealing details: his accent when he speaks Yiddish, and whether his gefilte fish is spicy or sweet. The presumed dividing line--the Mason-Dixon line of Jewish ancestry-- is between Lithuania/Latvia/Russia (spicy) and Poland/Germany/Western Europe (sweet). Of course, gefilte fish sweetened with sugar would be a relatively recent innovation, as historians tell us that sugar didn't come into common use until the 18th century.

When I was a kid growing up in the suburbs, the only gefilte fish to be had was either made from scratch by Bubby or bought in glass Manischewitz jars suspended in jelly. We would eat those Manischewitz fish balls for lunch along with hunks of matzoh spread with butter, much to the bewilderment of our non-Jewish neighbors. Even today, those isolated Jews in places like Flagstaff, Arizona or Spokane, Washington still rely on Manischewitz to supply them with bottled Yiddische nostalgia. Perhaps this is why Manischewitz still manages to sell over a million and a half of those jars every year, which, if you take a minute to do the math, works out to more than one jar for every ten Jews in the world!

But gefilte fish has come a long way, baby. In Jewish neighborhoods today, one can buy chopped fish from the fish man or frozen loaves from the supermarket (sweetened, unsweetened, and salmon). Upscale chefs tweak Mom's old gefilte recipes and pretentiously rename them *"quenelles de poisson"*; others color the defrosted fish with spinach and carrots and make tri-color terrines that look terribly impressive on a yom tov table. I myself am no less guilty of improvising; to please the Moroccan palates of my family, I buy unsweetened loaves of gefilte fish, defrost them, and reinvent them as fish balls served with tomato sauce and peppers or spicy chick peas.

My fish balls in tomato sauce, in fact, have become something of a signature dish, a most-requested recipe beloved even by my most-fussy daughter. My niece's three-year-old son once polished off no less than fifteen of them at one sitting. Not only are they warm and savory, but I recently stumbled upon a way to infuse them with spirituality as well as flavor—

That inspiration struck when I attended a small soiree hosted by a friend in honor of her mother's *yahrzeit.* Two congenial cousins of hers, Bobover Hasidic women from Boro Park, joined the reminiscing about my friend's departed mother, adding memories of their own mother. One of them mentioned that her mother's most mundane acts, like cooking for Shabbos, would be imbued with her close connection to the One Above. "When she would make her gefilte fish," the Bobover lady said, "she didn't make loaves like people do today; she made individual portions. And as she shaped each portion and put it into the pot, she would say a *bracha* for different people."

Well, a light went off in my head. Instead of standing in front of the stove mindlessly dropping fish balls into tomato sauce, I could use each one as the opportunity to say a *tefilah,* a prayer! The next Friday morning, I went into action. This fish ball, I prayed as I shaped a ball and threw it into the pot, was for a healthy baby for Devora bat Rachel. . . this one was for a shidduch for Sara bat Chana. . . this one for a *refuah shleimah* for Yosef David ben Nesha Mirel. . . this one for a release for Yaakov Yosef ben Raizel and then each of his fellow prisoners...

On the one hand, it felt kind of childish to be blessing fish balls, indulging in a kind of magical thinking not far removed from wishing on stars or blowing apart dandelion puffs. Then again, I thought, why not? Why not use an everyday act as an excuse to talk to Hashem, as a vehicle for prayer? I tried to remember not only to barrage Him with requests, but to count my blessings over the fish balls as well. My recipe makes enough fish balls for plenty of blessings as well as requests.

Of course, then I began to wonder about the celestial consequences of, say, my grand-nephew eating a fish ball blessed for Moshe ben Luna's *refuah shleima*, or my son eating a fish ball blessed for Tamo bat Esther's shidduch. Is it possible to invest a fish ball with spiritual *kavanot*? Does *hashgachah* then direct which person eats them as he performs the mitzvah of a Shabbos *seudah*, or can the brachas get mixed up randomly like a Chanukah gift grab-bag? What about all those tales where *tzaddikim* come back in the *gilgul* of a fish—did my gefilte fish loaf include a pike or mullet carrying a *neshama* that was destined to be turned into a fish ball blessed by a balabusta in Brooklyn?

Such lofty questions are beyond my humble ken. All I can tell you is that by Sunday night you won't find a single fish ball left in the fridge, because they really are very, very inspiring.

Moroccan Tricolor Fish Balls

A seudah including gefilte fish should always leave you feeling good and ge-filled! And not just in body, but in spirit as well.

Ingredients:

Sauce:

2 tbsp cooking oil
1/2 red pepper, cut into 1-inch dice
1/2 green pepper, cut into 1-inch dice
1/2 yellow pepper, cut into 1-inch dice
5 cloves garlic, chopped coarsely
1 jar favorite marinara sauce
2 tablespoons tomato paste
1 tsp. paprika
½ tsp hot paprika (or cayenne), or to taste

Fish balls:

1 loaf gefilte fish without sugar or sweetener, barely defrosted
½ c. bread crumbs
Salt, pepper
1 tsp. paprika
½ teaspoon turmeric
½ tsp hot paprika, or to taste
1 tbsp chopped parsley or cilantro

¼ c. chopped fresh parsley or cilantro for garnish (optional)

In a large, deep saucepan that has a lid, sauté the peppers in the oil over medium heat until softened, about seven-eight minutes. Add garlic and cook another two minutes. Add marinara sauce, tomato paste, paprika and hot paprika, and one cup of water to thin the sauce.

In a large mixing bowl, mix defrosted gefilte fish with the other ingredients. (Defrost only to the point that you can mix it and shape it into balls; if it gets too warm it will get sticky and hard to work with). Shape into walnut-sized balls with your fingers and add to the simmering tomato sauce and pepper mixture. Simmer, covered, for forty minutes, adding more water if sauce becomes too thick. Garnish with chopped parsley or cilantro and enjoy!

Recipes for Fresh Fish Fillets or Steaks

Since my poor husband knew not of gefilte fish, early on in our marriage I made sure to learn Moroccan ways of preparing fresh fish. These recipes create their own oil-based red sauce as they cook, which you then pour over the fish at the end. It would not be out of place in Moroccan cooking to raise the heat by adding a few of those little dried shata peppers to the pan, red pepper flakes, or some cut-up fresh hot peppers like jalapeno or ancho—just be judicious in case your guests don't share your asbestos tongue.

Eating fish has always been a tradition on Shabbos; the Gemara (Shabbos 118a) states that Rav Yehudah answered the question, "How should one delight in Shabbos?" by saying, "One should eat a large fish." The gematria, or Hebrew numerical value, of fish (*dag*) is seven, like the seventh day. For these reasons, many people have the custom to serve fish at all three of the Shabbos meals.

Moroccan Fish With Chick Peas

3 pounds salmon or whitefish (fillets or steaks—your call)
¼ cup oil
1 tablespoon tomato paste
½ teaspoon hot paprika or red pepper flakes (or to taste)
2 teaspoons sweet paprika

½ teaspoon chili powder
½ teaspoon turmeric
Salt, pepper
8 cloves garlic, coarsely chopped
1 onion, coarsely chopped
1 15-ounce can chick peas
1 small red pepper, cut into strips
1 small pepper of another color (orange, yellow or green, or a combination), cut in strips
¼ cup chopped cilantro (or parsley, but cilantro is more authentic)

Preheat oven to 350. Mix the oil, paprikas and turmeric in a large baking dish. Mix in the onion, garlic, and chickpeas. Now roll the rinsed pieces of fish in the spiced oil to coat. Sprinkle fish pieces with salt and pepper and top with the strips of cut peppers.

Cover and bake for half an hour; uncover and continue to bake another thirty minutes or so, basting the fish with the oil and adding a little water if it starts to dry out. Garnish with chopped cilantro and enjoy.

This can also be cooked on the stove, which is a faster method. Saute the onion, garlic, and peppers in oil; add the tomato paste and spices and sear the fish in the oil, flesh side down. Turn fish over after a few minutes, add the herbs and chick peas and about half a cup of water. Salt and pepper to taste. Let it simmer about 15 minutes until done and garnish with more herbs.

Moroccan Fish Mamy Gisele

2-3 pounds fish steaks or filets
¼ cup oil

1 onion, chopped
4 cloves garlic, chopped
1 large tomato, chopped, or two small ones
2 teaspoons tomato paste
2 teaspoons sweet paprika
½ teaspoon chili powder
¼ teaspoon turmeric
Salt, pepper
¼ cup finely chopped walnuts

Heat oil in a large saucepan over medium high heat. Add onions, garlic, paprika, turmeric and tomato paste, and sauté until onions are transparent. Add the chopped tomato and sauté a few minutes more. Now add the fish, turning once to coat and sprinkling with salt and pepper.

Add ¾ cup water and simmer the fish, partially covered, about 30 minutes, until most of the water is evaporated and fish is well cooked through (add water if it starts to burn or gets dried out), basting occasionally. Top with the chopped walnuts and baste again during the last few minutes of cooking.

Chapter 6

Soup of the Evening, Beautiful Soup

WHEN WE ARE little and lack language to fix our impressions in memory, we tend to retain experiences as pure sensory impressions. A certain image, smell or taste may become forever linked in our minds with a particular person or place. The classic example of this, of course, is the celebrated passage in Proust's *Swann's Way*, in which the protagonist takes a bite of a *madeleine* cookie and is immediately transported into pages upon pages' worth of rich, sweeping recollections of his childhood.

My own childhood memories took place in rather less *chichi* settings than the French countryside. . .the Bronx, for example. Rather than delicate *madeleines*, what evokes childhood recollections for me is the taste and smell of a clear, fragrant chicken soup. I have quite vivid memories of the weekend visits my family used to make from our home in the Philadelphia suburbs to my grandparents' apartment in the Bronx, pilgrimages of filial piety to a neighborhood that was rapidly turning from bad to worse.

As a child I always waited excitedly for that first glimpse

from the New Jersey Turnpike of the New York City skyline, glinting far away in the sun like the Emerald City in Oz. Then just minutes afterward the car would dive into the depths of the Holland Tunnel, with its otherworldly lights and unnatural quiet, broken only by the whooshing of cars. That was an experience that simultaneously fascinated and frightened me: When would the tunnel end? What if we broke down in the middle? Would we come out the other end?—fears that, by the way, occasionally resurface ever since spending 9/11 within sighting distance of the disaster.

When finally, to my private relief, we emerged into light, it was to find ourselves reborn into another world altogether. New York seemed terribly exotic to a kid used to the tranquility and homogeneity of the suburbs. In the Bronx there were shouts and the honking of horns heard, as I lay on a canvas folding cot, until late into the night and again early in the gray New York mornings; the powerful rumble of the subways and the multicolored faces of the people who rode them; the bakeries where old Jewish salesladies in hairnets barked at customers who ordered their onion rolls too slowly, and the Barton's store near Yankee Stadium where my parents always stocked up on a box of dark chocolate almond bark, a precious commodity as yet unavailable in the uncivilized wastelands of Levittown.

We would circle my grandmother's neighborhood looking for parking before ascending with all our baggage (including the two clanking folding cots for the kids to sleep on) across the apartment courtyard where my father once played stickball. In the dark, cavernous lobby, a creaking elevator would lift us up two flights to a tiled landing where every footstep left ringing echos down the hall and our parents shushed us and warned us not to run. Everything in that building seemed ancient to me: the creaky wooden floors in the apartment, the smell of mothballs in the closet, the fire escapes outside the bedroom window, the framed, forbidding photograph of my great-grand-father in his hat and long beard. The closest thing to modernity was a capricious black and white TV set where we kids watched a fuzzy-imaged Rocky and Bullwinkle and my father would pass the afternoon with the baseball game.

We kids knew which apartment to run to from the elevator, but even so we could have easily picked it out simply from the strong smell of chicken soup wafting through the door upon our arrival. My grandmother always had "lunch" waiting for us when we came, lunch that was really a European midday dinner rather than an American lunch, complete with chicken soup, chicken, vegetables, and a plain, slightly sweet homemade coffee cake that I found uninteresting as a child and would probably adore today.

Every Jewish kid thinks *his* grandmother makes the world's best chicken soup, but mine, of course, *really* did. It was tremendously clear and golden, and she made her own noodles and soup "mandlen," little balls made of chicken fat and flour and eggs that we threw in the soup and loved for their rich eggy flavor. My mother claims my grandmother also made delicious potato soup and some other good soups as well, but it is that chicken soup that stayed with me as the gold standard of soup (with apologies to my mother, who makes a pretty terrific chicken soup herself). In fact, I am convinced that if today I have achieved any competence as a soup-maker, it was either passed on through a special Jewish soup-making chromosome or bestowed by my grandmother through some sort of mystical soup-making blessing. (In fairy tales the fairy godmothers shower gifts of beauty and song on baby princesses, but we Jewish princesses are more likely to get the gift of making chicken soup.)

My children all inherited my love of chicken soup, so I

make it for them from time to time, fussing over it as my grand-mother did—making it a day early, straining it, skimming the fat, adding vegetables. I would make my grandmother's soup *mandlen* as well, except that unfortunately, her recipe left this world along with her. The puffy store-bought balls I've seen don't bear the slightest resemblance to her denser, crispier version. On the other hand, I'm sure Grandma's recipe included generous quantities of home-rendered chicken fat, which is something I have never stocked in my pantry; like most members of this health-conscious generation I throw out what-ever chicken fat I skim off the top of my chicken soups, on the premise it's better left sticking to the sides of the garbage can than sticking to our arteries. (My grandmother, on the other hand, always kept chicken fat on hand in such abundant quan-tity that whenever we took leave of her apartment she'd insist that my mother take home several mayonnaise jars full of it. My mother always accepted these offerings graciously, but as soon as we got into the car could be heard muttering under her breath to my father, "Now what in heaven's name am I supposed to do with all this *schmaltz*?").

Alas, what a disappointment, many years later, when I found that my enthusiasm for chicken soup was not shared by my adoring spouse! My husband was puzzled and incredulous that I could work up so much enthusiasm over what looked to him like so much flavored hot water. Moroccans, I quickly learned, like a soup you can stand a spoon up in, preferably with a few meaty bones throw in. The typical *Moroccan* soup consists of vegetables and/or beans generally cooked with meat bones and then pureed, resulting in a soup that is smooth, tasty and nourishing. The flavor comes from herbs like garlic, onions, leeks and cilantro, spices like saffron, thyme and pepper, and meat when desired. Needless to say, it didn't take me long to develop a strong attachment to these soups as well, and they have become (even more than chicken soup) our standard fare for Friday nights.

In principle, this sort of vegetable soup is about the easiest thing in the world to make: throw water, vegetables and bones into a pot, boil away for an hour or two, and puree the whole thing by sticking in one of those electric immersion blenders, nifty gadgets that will set you back a whole ten dollars or so if you catch a sale. (Take the bones out, if any, before you start whirring your blender around the pot!)

But how many carrots? How many cups of water? The novice soup-maker wants the quantities spelled out. So I find myself obliged to confess: I never measure when I make soup. For one thing, I just can't be bothered; to the dismay of certain family members, I am not much of a detail person. Secondly, it takes away a lot of the challenge and all of the creativity and fun. Thirdly, I no longer need to! Not any more, folks, not since the day I invented:

The Lazy Person's No-Measure Soup Technique

The Lazy Person's No-Measure approach to soup-making begins with the principle that almost every soup—vegetable, anyway—starts with a base of a couple of carrots, a couple of ribs of celery, an onion, and a clove or two of garlic. (Sometimes you don't want the celery; sometimes a leek is in order as well). These ingredients give the soup flavor, especially if sautéed in a little oil before adding in other ingredients and the liquids. Hence the first step in my soup creation process is to sauté these vegetables for five minutes or so, adding in meat or bones to brown once the vegetables have softened, before adding any other vegetables and liquids.

Here is the next soup-making trick. Most Moroccan soups are pureed, and you want to have the right balance of water or broth to vegetables in order to be sure your puree is neither too thin nor too thick. How does one achieve this balance without measuring? The trick is to start the puree process *before* the soup even gets cooked.

What you need to do is chop all your vegetables in a food processor *before* they go into the pot, including those initial carrots, onions, and celery (use the steel knife/chopping blade, and leave them coarsely chopped; too fine and they will scorch more quickly). Once you've sautéed those, you chop all the other vegetables in the processor and add them to the pot, along with enough water or broth so that all the pieces are covered and floating loosely in the liquid. This allows you to make a soup from, say, two or eight sweet potatoes without having to break your head worrying about adjusting proportions of vegetable to liquid. Just put in enough water to cover the vegetables comfortably, and add spices to taste, and you're in business.

This procedure will make a vegetarian soup cook very quickly, in only about half an hour or so, because there are no large chunks of vegetables to heat through (a meat soup will require more time, because the meat has to cook until tender). Once the soup has finished cooking you take out any bones and stick in your handy immersion blender to puree the soup. It should end up at just about the right consistency. (If it's too thick, add a little water; if it's too thin, instant potato flakes can help repair the damages.) Then put your meat or bones back in.

Of course, this will all seem much clearer if you try it out with an actual recipe. Here's one of my Moroccan standards, a vegetable soup with wonderful flavors:

Moroccan Meat-and-Potato-Leek Soup

Start this soup by putting about two large carrots, a couple of ribs of celery, an onion, a few cloves of garlic, and a leek (well-cleaned, white part only) into your trusty food processor. Chop them coarsely with the steel knife and add to a soup pot whose bottom you have covered with a little olive oil and a bay leaf (regular oil with do just fine also). Saute these vegetables until they are softened, about five minutes, and add in a few meaty bones or marrow bones. Brown the bones with the vegetables. Now put about eight medium potatoes, peeled and chopped in your processor, into the pot. Add enough water so that all the pieces are covered and floating loosely in the liquid, and bring to a boil. While the soup is heating up, add the spices: salt and pepper, half a teaspoon of turmeric, another half teaspoon of thyme. I like to add a few cubes or a couple of tablespoons of chicken consommé powder to give more flavor (if you're a purist, substitute real or canned chicken broth for some or all of the water). The adventurous and those with gourmet aspirations might want to try adding a few threads of saffron as well to add a subtle, slightly grassy fragrance.

Let your soup simmer for about an hour and a half, stirring occasionally because the pieces of potato tend to sink to the bottom and will burn if you don't check the soup from time to time. When the soup has cooked long enough to soften the meat on the bones, take it off the stove and let it cool slightly. Add about one third cup chopped cilantro (you can substitute parsley if you dislike the distinctive taste of cilantro, but cilantro gives a more authentic Moroccan flavor). Take out the bones, take out your immersion blender, and whir your soup into a puree. (If you like your soups "piece-y," as my kids put it, you can leave it half-pureed.) At this point you might want to break bits of meat off the bones and throw them back into the soup along with the bones themselves; that way everybody gets to have a little meat in their soup.

During Pesach, we makes this soup for the Seder nights

with fava beans, which are softer and more edible when the outer hull of the bean is peeled.

The Lazy Person's No-Measure Soup Technique lends itself to making pureed soups from all sorts of vegetables, alone or in combination. Sweet potatoes make wonderful pureed soup; so do zucchini. Beets can be added to meat and vegetable combinations for borscht. I find soup is the ultimate way to use up the slightly-wilted vegetables that nobody wants to eat any more but don't yet merit the garbage pail either; just sneak them into a puree and your finicky kids will be none the wiser. (In some soups, however, like carrot soup, using fresh vegetables will make an appreciable difference in the flavor.) When left on the thick side, pureed soups also make terrific homemade baby food. Just leave out any strong spices so that baby doesn't get indigestion and keep you up all night with colic!

I hope all this has inspired you to create some "soup-er" recipes of your own. Just one final note: there were a few crucial ingredients that made my grandmother's soups so special and with which I try to imbue my own. The first was a deep respect for tradition that dictated that the food be prepared with strictly kosher ingredients in a kitchen that, in my grandmother's case, boasted red-striped towels for meat and blue-striped towels for dairy, not to mention *pushkas* for the Hebrew Home of the Sages and orphanages in Israel. The second ingredient, surely a holdover from many years of new-immigrant and Depression-era poverty, was the obsessive notion that children should be well-fed—stuffed if necessary—to be sure they grow up strong and healthy. (This, unfortunately, drove all of us a little crazy as unsolicited third helpings were dumped onto our plates, followed by mournful sighs if we didn't finish them.)

Lastly, and most importantly, there was the fierce love of family that permeated everything she prepared for us. That love ensured that the food she cooked nourished us not only in body but right into our souls. It is many years later, and many years since she left us, and in my own life I have both gone more deeply into the Judaism she loved and segued into a Sephardic heritage she barely knew existed. But those bowls of chicken soup are still nourishing me. Somewhere, someplace very deep in the core of my being, her soups are still generating warmth and strength.

(In memory of my grandmother Netty Greenfield a"h)

Chapter 7

A Chicken in Every Pot (It Must be Shabbat!)

Chicken soup is the quintessential Shabbat dish for European Jews, and a quintessential comfort food universally. But an unfortunate consequence of serving chicken soup is often that the family gets served bland boiled chicken for the main course.

That's how my father grew up, and even though my grandmother made delicious chicken soup, he could never abide the boiled chicken that followed. Over half a century later, he still abhors the stuff.

One culinary step above boiled chicken is baked chicken, the American standard. The first chicken I ever cooked, at age nine and with the assistance of my mother, came from a children's cookbook recipe that suggested rolling the chicken pieces in crushed potato chips before baking (very appealing to kids, a bit disgusting to adults). Today, I rather like baked breaded chicken and sauce-basted baked chicken, but my significant other begs to differ. He always judges it either undercooked or dry. The Moroccan way with chicken is to braise it: sauté an onion and/or garlic, brown the chicken, add vegetables or fruit, some spices and water, and let'er rip until the water has cooked down and thickened into sauce.

This creates a chicken that's moist and falling off the bone, while the chicken and vegetables or fruits become infused with each other's flavor. Mounded onto a platter, glazed with the thickened juices and surrounded by the cooked fruit or vegetables, it makes a stunning impression.

The chicken with apricots recipe that follows is based on one of my mother-in-law's recipes. It has a special place in my heart, not only as a family favorite but because I once entered it into a magazine recipe contest in the hopes of winning the first prize, a badly needed new stove. I didn't win the stove, but I won second prize, which was a set of new silverware (which I also needed). And after that the editor called and asked me to write a regular food column for her newspaper.

The second recipe, chicken with chickpeas, is a dish I invented in desperation during one of those back-to-back three-day holiday-plus-Shabbat marathons, during which I'd used every recipe I'd ever encountered and just had to make something *new*. Turns out everybody loved it, so we designated this innovation a "keeper."

Moroccan Chicken with Apricots

Ingredients:

3 tbsp. cooking oil
1 onion, diced
1 clove garlic, chopped
1 plum tomato, diced
1 chicken (about 3 pounds), cut into eighths
Salt, pepper
1 tsp. turmeric

1 tsp. cinnamon
½ tsp. ginger
1 ½ c. chicken broth or water (you can make "broth" with one
teaspoon consommé powder and hot water)
2 cups dried apricots

In a large, deep saucepan that has a cover, begin to saute the onions in the oil over medium heat. When onions are transparent, add the garlic and turmeric, stirring to blend. Now add the chicken to the pot and let it brown on both sides, 3-4 minutes a side, until it turns golden brown. While it is browning, add the tomato and sprinkle the chicken with the salt, pepper, cinnamon, and ginger.

Once it has finished browning, add the apricots and chicken broth to the pot. Now simmer it, partially covered, for one hour, until most of the liquid is absorbed and the apricots and chicken are soft and infused with each other's flavor.

Nice served over couscous or rice.

Chicken With Chick Peas

2 tablespoons oil
1 small onion, diced
8 cloves garlic, chopped coarsely
1 chicken cut in eighths (about 3 pounds)
Salt, pepper
1 teaspoon paprika
½ teaspoon hot paprika (or to taste)
½ teaspoon turmeric
½ teaspoon chili powder
1 teaspoon cumin
1 can chickpeas
¼ cup chopped cilantro (optional)

Heat oil in a large skillet over medium-high heat; add onions and sauté until starting to brown. Add the turmeric and the garlic pieces and mix well, then place the chicken pieces in the oil to brown. As they sauté, sprinkle the chicken with half of all the other spices and cook until golden brown, about three minutes; turn and repeat on the other side. Add the can of chick peas and 1 ½ cups water or chicken broth. Simmer, partially covered, for about an hour, until the chicken is tender and cooked through and most of the liquid has evaporated. Garnish with the cilantro.

Also good with chunks of potato added in.

Chapter 8

Cholent: The Ultimate One-Pot Shabbos Dish

AFTER WINE for Kiddush and challah for blessing the bread, surely the food that most completely captures the essence of Shabbat is cholent. By eating a hot dish for Shabbat lunch, we affirm our commitment to observing *Torah sheba'al peh,* the Rabbinic laws that permit the consumption (although not the preparation) of hot food. This practice historically distinguished mainstream Judaism from the Karaites, who rejected the rabbinic tradition and ate only cold food on Shabbat.

Cholent is just the ticket to filling stomachs growling after a long morning in shul, not to mention satisfying the extra appetite endowed upon us by the presence of a hungry *neshama yeteirah*—the "additional soul" we are said to acquire on Shabbat. (Of course, as the wags note, our *neshama yeteirah* always slips away at the close of Shabbat, leaving us with all those extra calories!)

Jews have been eating cholent-like stews on Shabbat for as long as anyone can remember. Meat was not always as readily available as it is today, and so, like many dishes from poorer countries, it is based largely on legumes, with smaller amounts of meat thrown in for flavor. In the Middle East, those legumes were often garbanzos; in Europe, beans and barley. Legumes hold up well against many hours of cooking—they require it, in fact. The bad news is that afterwards they require almost as many hours of digestion! Which, of course, makes cholent the ideal inducement to a Shabbos nap. . .

There are those who claim the word "cholent" comes from the Old French "*chaud-lent*," meaning "hot—slow." But I prefer the suggestion of those who claim it comes from modern English: "shul—end!" At any rate, the name inspired musician Country Yossi to write a whole song dedicated to "ch-ch-ch-cholent," in which he claims that one day, "Cholent-powered rockets will send people to the moon!" Such is the amazing power of cholent, assuming the rocket doesn't fall asleep and topple over from its own weight before takeoff.

In the old communities of Europe and the Middle East, many people didn't have the cooking facilities to keep their cholents warm for so many hours. They would send their cholents to cook in the community oven until the following day, when everyone would come to reclaim their pots. There were those who sealed their pots shut with a bready crust, others who packed their cholents with kishka and kugel. I know people who grew up with this type of system in Morocco, and insist that slow cooking in a bakery oven gives the cholent a special flavor. When I see clay-pot roasters touted in trendy cooking catalogs as a unique way to bring out extra flavor in food, I think of cholents roasted in bakery ovens.

People get very attached to their family cholents; there are those who insist on leaving it soupy, while others like it on the pasty side. Then there is the *blech* [stovetop flame tamer] versus crock pot debate for letting it simmer all night. Personally, I found my family outgrew even the six-quart crock pots after awhile, and the crock pots gave me less control over the heat (when I left the thing on high all Shabbos the cholent burned, but when I left it on low it never seemed to cook down enough).

For those using the *blech*, there is always the anxiety: will it burn? Will it come out well-done enough, or be too watery? My husband has been known to wake me up in the middle of the night to whisper romantically: "I think the cholent is burning— can you go move it on the *blech*?" But that's mild compared to another friend who claims he barely sleeps Friday nights because he's so worried his precious cholent will burn!

Over the years, my husband has developed two theories about cholent. The first is that cholent has the power to preserve Jewish identity when all other ties have been severed. Growing up in Morocco, he knew families who had become very Europeanized, and yet, even as they would go to the beach on Shabbos, would pack up their *daffina* (the Moroccan version of cholent) and bring it along for lunch. I once heard Rabbi Paysach Krohn tell the story of a young man who had become estranged from Judaism, but was drawn back when the smell of cholent wafting out of a shul one Saturday morning enticed him to reenter the shul and, ultimately, religious life in general.

My husband's second theory is that a disdain for cholent is dangerous and could be the early warning sign of a general disdain for Judaism. Personally, I'm not sure the second theory is always true. I never much cared for beans, so I don't love cholent, although I do like *daffina* (which uses garbanzos). But I have to admit that during my pregnancies I couldn't abide even *daffina*—that *daffina* smell permeating the house for twenty-four hours left me incapable of eating it. (Maybe it's because I was always the one left to scrub out the icky pot when I burned it!)

There are about as many versions of cholent as there are stars in the sky. The proof of this comes from the many descendents of the Biblical Abraham, who was promised his descendents would be as numerous as the stars, many of whom today live in Israel. A "cholent contest" was held several years ago at the Dan Panorama Hotel in Haifa, and there were 131 semi-finalists! The winner, a certain Mrs. Esther Israel of Kfar Saba, produced a very original cholent that included beef, chicken, semolina dumplings, stuffed vegetables and spinach, and perhaps the kitchen sink as well. She told the judges that if she only had more time, she would have added homemade kishka or stuffed grape leaves as well! (That sounds rather like gilding the lily, but hey, who could imagine that cholent could, as it were, go for baroque?)

Obviously, most of us produce cholents that are much simpler; in fact, the basic cholent recipe is straightforward enough so that, according to my children, no young man leaves yeshiva without having learned how to produce a respectable facsimile of cholent. Boys being boys, they have also been known to experiment, adding everything from ketchup to barbecue sauce to Coca-Cola to the mix (rather a far cry from the dry red wines and duck *confit* recommended in those revamped, upscale cholent-cum-*cassoulet* recipes!).

But just thinking about cholent makes me sleepy, so I will bid you cho-long, with a wish that your cholents always cook perfectly and taste like that little piece of the World-To-Come they're supposed to evoke!

Daffina

3 tablespoons oil
2 onions, chopped
1 head garlic, four cloves separated off
1 ½ cups dried chick peas, soaked in water overnight
2 pounds flanken or kolichel
2-3 marrow bones

1-2 knee bones, if desired
2 sweet potatoes
4 pounds baby red potatoes
5-6 eggs
1 ½ cups rice (I like basmati)
1 cup wheat berries (*chittah*)
Salt, pepper, paprika, turmeric, cumin, hot paprika, dash cinnamon (optional)
Optional: ½ teaspoon saffron dissolved in one large glass of boiling water

Heat the oil in a large pot and sauté the onions, adding in the head of garlic cut side down (outer skin removed, top sliced off as for roasting). When onions are transparent, add the meat and bones (reserve one marrow bone for later) and brown them. Remove about 1/3 cup of browned onions from the pot and reserve.

Add the drained chickpeas, the sweet potatoes and potatoes, half the saffron water if desired, and about a quart of water. Spice with salt, pepper, about two teaspoons of turmeric and a tablespoon of paprika. When the mixture begins to boil, add the eggs and turn the flame down to a simmer.

Make the rice: Put the rice in a small bowl; add one chopped clove of garlic, a teaspoon of oil, salt, pepper, ½ teaspoon turmeric, a tiny dash of cinnamon if desired, the reserved chopped onions, and one reserved marrow bone. Add one cup saffron water and 1 and 1/3 cups water, or 2 and 1/3 cups water. (Add any remaining saffron water to the daffina pot). Mix and pour into a plastic roasting bag; knot the bag and throw it into the pot. N.B.: Watch the bag as your daffina begins to heat up; they often swell from the heat and pressure. Pierce a couple of tiny holes in it to allow steam to escape. Otherwise the bag may break, the rice will fall into the daffina and you will end up with cholent instead! The same principle applies to the bag of wheat.

Make the wheat: In a bowl, mix the wheat grains, two chopped cloves of garlic, salt and pepper, ¼ teaspoon turmeric, ¼ teaspoon hot paprika (or to taste), ½ teaspoon paprika, ½ teaspoon cumin, and 1 cup of wheat. Add about 1 2/3 cups water. Pour into a roasting bag and add to pot, piercing bag.

Add enough water to the pot so that all the ingredients are covered. Boil a couple of hours before Shabbat and leave it simmering on your blech overnight. In Morocco, families would bring their daffinas to community ovens overnight and the kids would fetch them after shul in the morning.

Part Two

Holidays

Chapter 9

Rosh Hashanah With Rosh Keves: the Sephardi Rosh Hashanah Seder

BEFORE I GOT MARRIED, I thought a Seder was something that happened only once a year, something that necessarily had to do with horseradish, matzoh and slavery. So imagine my surprise when the first September of our married life rolled around, and I discovered that in Sephardi homes you have to make a whole Seder for Rosh Hashanah too!

I grew up with Rosh Hashanah traditions like dipping apples in honey, buying raisin challahs in lieu of plain, and eating the head of a fish and carrots (read *tzimmes*, which as a child made me shudder). But the Sephardic Rosh Hashanah Seder involves a rather more elaborate range of ceremonial foods, some of which I had never heard of and others I had formerly never had the least inclination to sample, let alone prepare. My shopping list, I soon discovered, was to include the following items: dates, leeks, Swiss chard, black-eyed peas, gourd, quince, pomegranates, apples, and last but not least, the head of a sheep. . . "*Wait* a minute," I said to my husband. "A *sheep?*"

"Well, I don't know if we can get it here in New York," he

65

shrugged. "But in Morocco we used to serve the whole head, teeth and all."

In Morocco, even today, a family who needs meat for yom tov does not sally forth to the local kosher supermarket and choose a pre-soaked, pre-salted package neatly wrapped up with a foam tray and cellophane. No, they have to buy the entire beast, which the *shochet* slaughters and cuts up for them, and then (this according to my sister-in-law in Marrakech) they spend the better part of a day soaking and salting, dividing those chunks into portions, putting them into labeled plastic bags and organizing them in the freezer. The upshot of this is that they eat every kosher part of the animal, from tongue to tripe to kidneys—and, of course, the head.

I have since discovered that my local supermarket, which has a large Sephardic clientele, makes sure to offer every year before Rosh Hashanah a product euphemistically entitled "lamb cheeks." That they are part of the lamb's head is evidenced by, yes, the occasionally teeth still clinging to the jawbone (guaranteed to provoke squeals of disgust from your kids). But every year I buy several packs of them and cook them up for the holiday, and lo and behold, they are actually very delicious. After all, it's really just lamb meat, and the same kids who originally shrieked with horror can later be found coming to blows over the last bits of meat left on the bone.

As for the other ingredients, until I finally figured out where all the Sephardic grocery stores were, my husband and I spent ridiculous amounts of time and energy scouring the neighborhood in a scavenger hunt to find them. I still remember wandering glassy-eyed between endless rows of pedestrian potatoes and carrots, desperately in search of the ever-elusive quinces, blackeyed peas, and Swiss chard. It was nerve-wracking to find myself only several hours away from *yom tov* and unable to find half the ingredients I needed! On one occasion I am quite sure a befuddled store owner gave me bok choy when I asked him for Swiss chard, and in my ignorance I cooked it up and served it anyway.

My Sephardic prayer book explains the reasons we eat these unusual foods. We eat gourd, *kra'a*, asking Hashem "*sh'tikra roa g'zar dineinu*"—that He should tear up evil judgments against us. We ask that our merits increase like *rubeya*, blackeyed peas (*sheyirbu zechuyoteinu k'rubeya*). The Swiss chard, *silka*, is so that "*sheyistalku oyveinu v'soneinu*"— Hashem should remove our foes and enemies. And that famous *rosh keves* not only expresses our wish to be "the head and not the tail," but recalls the ram of *akeidat Yitzhak,* the binding of Isaac.

I eventually found ways to prepare all the exotic ingredients I bought for our Rosh Hashanah Seder, and would spend the better part of a morning simply cooking Seder foods. But once I had exhausted myself with those, it would dawn on me that I still had at least four yom tov *meals* to prepare! *Oy vey!*

Fortunately, over the years I developed several standard menus that make the planning easier, mostly sweet dishes (for a "sweet" New Year) like chicken with apricots or beef with prunes. One of my family's favorite recipes is a squash soup that my mother-in-law maintains is the custom in Marrakech for the first night of Rosh Hashanah. Just about everybody loves this soup for its warming combination of meaty marrow bones and sweet squash; in fact, once on a lark I sent the recipe to the now-defunct, once-hoity-toity *Gourmet* magazine, and even *Gourmet* saw fit to publish it. My mother-in-law claims this soup is excellent for nursing mothers—the vitamins in the squash and the iron and fat in the bones can't help but enrich the milk. And if you should unexpectedly find yourself with last-minute extra guests due to, say, your cousin's refrigerator breaking down an hour before the holiday and her deciding to take her whole family over to *you*, fear not: this soup is easy enough to stretch. Just pop in one or two of those 12-ounce packages of frozen winter squash and a little water, and it will be every bit as delicious.

Rosh Hashanah Soup (Squash and Marrow Bone Soup)

2 tablespoons oil
2 onions
2 cloves garlic
3 carrots, peeled and cut in chunks
1 package marrow bones (about five or six medium-sized bones)
1 large or two small butternut squash, peeled and cut in chunks
1 teaspoon turmeric
1 teaspoon cinnamon
Water or chicken broth
Salt, pepper

Chop the onions, carrots and garlic coarsely in a food processor. Heat the oil in your soup pot and sauté these chopped vegetables in the oil for about five minutes, adding the marrow bones to brown as they cook. Now chop the squash in the processor as well and add to the pot along with enough chicken broth or water (which you may flavor with a tablespoon of chicken consommé powder) so that all the vegetables are covered and floating loosely in the pot. Add in spices, and simmer for about an hour.

Allow soup to cool a bit, remove the bones, and puree the soup until creamy (I use an immersion blender, or you can puree it in batches in a processor.) If it's too thick, add a little water; if your squash was not so ripe, you may want to heighten the sweetness with a little sugar.

This should serve at least ten people. Distribute the marrow bones to the shameless carnivores in your family!

Rosh Keves (Lamb Cheeks) With Gourd

2 lamb cheeks
2 tablespoons oil
1/2 teaspoon turmeric (curcum)
2 large onions, cut into chunks
2-3 cloves garlic, coarsely chopped
4 carrots, cut in two-inch chunks
1 small butternut squash, peeled and cut into one-inch chunks
½ cup prunes or raisins
½ teaspoon cinnamon
Salt, pepper

Heat the oil over medium heat in a large saucepan, mixing in the turmeric to color it yellow. Add the onions and cook until they are transparent and beginning to brown. Now add the lamb cheeks and brown on both sides. Add the carrots, cinnamon, salt and pepper, and sauté for a minute or two. Add two cups of water and simmer, partially covered, for about forty-five minutes. Add the squash and prunes and simmer another twenty minutes or so, until the meat is tender and most of the water is evaporated (if it cooks down too much, add more water to prevent burning). If you love chickpeas, you can add a can after browning the meat.

Each lamb cheek provides enough meat for four to five people to have a little taste. This gives you squash for one "*yehi ratzon*" as well as the *rosh keves* for the other.

Chapter 10

Preparing for Yom Kippur, Gastronomically Speaking

YOM KIPPUR IS the moment of the year when we devote ourselves to self-evaluation, repenting and confessing. So before discussing Yom Kippur any further, I will come forth with a small confession: I don't cook much Sephardic food when it comes to my family's *erev* Yom Kippur meal.

First of all, the sages advise us not to eat spicy foods before the fast. Right away that rules out more than a few Sephardic specialties, which tend to have substantially more zing than their Eastern European counterparts. My second reason for preferring to serve Ashkenazi-style cuisine is that I've read that athletes who are preparing for strenuous events like marathons follow a regime called carbohydrate loading: they stuff themselves full of energy-releasing, carbohydrate-rich foods like spaghetti and bread and potatoes and cake.

So I figure that before we embark on the marathon prayer sessions and other physical challenges of Yom Kippur, it would behoove us spiritual athletes to do some serious carbohydrate loading as well. And in order to accomplish this, Ashkenazi cooking fits the bill just perfectly: think matzoh balls, potato and noodle kugels, and apple or sponge cakes and rugelach. I help my nearest and dearest load up on carbs before Yom Kippur with a meal full of matzoh ball soup and roast chicken and two or three kinds of kugel and cake.

And yet, we couldn't possibly eschew *all* things Sephardic. One North African tradition we always manage to fit in is to make special challah rolls for the occasion, stuffed with a mixture of raisins and almonds for a sweet year. The kids like them because we paint the tops with egg and sugar and a few toasted, sliced almonds, and everybody gets his or her own individual roll placed next to his plate.

Some Moroccans, especially those from the Spanish-speaking northern regions around Tangiers, make a sort of sweet eggplant spread called *al-beraniya* for the meal preceding the fast. Sweet eggplant? I know, that sounds about as funny to the Ashkenazi sensibility as sweet gefilte fish sounds to the Sephardic. But North Africans will take just about any fruit or vegetable and make it into a "jam" by cooking it a very long time with a lot of sugar. I have seen carrot jam, eggplant jam, watermelon rind jam, grapefruit and *etrog* (citron) jam. My mother-in-law buys tiny little eggplants and cooks them slowly with sugar until they look like large figs and taste equally sweet and fruity, oozing syrup on the plate. One of my Moroccan neighbors once invited us for dessert in her family's succah and put out at least five different kinds of these colorful homemade "jams" for us to sample.

I can't admit to being wholly enamored of these jam concoctions, as they're so sugar-laden they seem to me to be so much diabetes served up on a plate. Perhaps they stood in for candy in times when processed candies, kosher or otherwise, were unavailable; you certainly can't eat more than a few bites of them. But the *al-beraniya* is somewhat lighter on the sugar (some recipes call for honey instead) while being heavier on the eggplant and oil. Still a stick-to-your-ribs spread to see you through the fast.

People who are hopeless coffee addicts like me like to grab that one last cup of brew before the fast, in the hopes of prolonging the onset of those debilitating caffeine withdrawal headaches—and then we can't wait to break the fast with a cup of the old java as well. In the days before pareve milk substitutes, the North African Jews came up with something even better: a sort of nonalcoholic zabaglione that sweetens and lightens the brew. It takes a few minutes of beating time, but it's worth a try. You beat egg yolks with sugar until the mixture is thick and almost white, and then spoon a dollop into black coffee with a sprinkling of cinnamon. It's quite tasty and is a North African tradition for after the Yom Kippur fast.

People used to wish each other, "Have an easy fast" before Yom Kippur. Today they give it a New Age spin and say, "Have a meaningful fast." At any rate, those twenty-five hours of fasting should leave us both physically and spiritually cleaned out, ready to start the new year fresh and uplifted.

Al-Beraniya

2 pounds eggplants (about 2 large or 3 small)
Cooking oil
½ cup sugar
½ cup honey
½ teaspoon cinnamon
¼ teaspoon ginger (optional)
Dash of salt and pepper
½ cup roasted sesame seeds or roasted chopped almonds

Wash eggplants, cut off the ends, and peel off a few wide strips of peel so that the eggplants look striped. Cut them crosswise into ½ inch slices. Heat the oil in a heavy-bottomed skillet until piping hot; fry the slices until golden brown.

Drain any excess oil from the pan and put the fried slices back in with the sugar and honey. Simmer together, stirring from time to time, for at least an hour, until the eggplant slices have fallen apart and reduced to the consistency of jam. Add the spices and cook ten minutes more. Add sesame seeds or almonds and serve.

Yom Kippur Rolls

Dough:
2 packets dry yeast
2 teaspoons sugar
1 cup warm water
6 cups flour
6 tablespoons sugar
2 teaspoons salt
2 eggs
2/3 cup water
2/3 cup oil

Filling:
¾ cup raisins
½ cup sliced almonds
¼ teaspoon turmeric
1 tablespoon oil
Topping: 1 beaten egg, sugar, sliced almonds

Proof the yeast with the sugar in the warm water; let sit until foamy, about three minutes. In the bowl of a mixer, combine the dry ingredients. Add the yeast mixture and mix well; now add the eggs, water and oil and knead well with a dough hook or by hand (this recipe can also be kneaded in a food processor—let it go for one minute--but you need to halve it and do it twice unless you want to blow the motor on your machine).

Let dough rise until double; punch it down (you can let it rise twice if that fits your schedule better). Divide dough into twelve balls.

Mix the filling ingredients in a bowl. Take each dough ball and divide it in half, shaping each half into a patty. Poke a well in one half and fill with a tablespoon of filling. Cover with the other half and pinch edges to seal, then crimp with the tines of a fork. Repeat with the other rolls.

Cover and place on greased baking sheets to rise until doubled. Brush tops with beaten egg, sprinkle with sugar and a few sliced almonds. Bake at 350 degrees about twenty minutes, until golden brown.

Moroccan Pareve Coffee Cream

4 egg yolks
4 tablespoons sugar
Cinnamon

Beat the egg yolks for a minute or two with an electric mixture. Continue mixing, gradually adding the sugar. Beat for about five minutes, until the mixture is very thick and light-colored. Spoon about a tablespoon of the "cream" into cups of hot black coffee, sprinkle with cinnamon and serve.

Chapter 11

Stylish Soups for Sukkoth

My husband is a perfectionist who invests himself three hundred percent when he commits to a project, and nowhere is this more true than when it comes to his sukkah, the little "hut" Jews build to dwell in for the holiday of Sukkoth. No flimsy canvas-and-aluminum pole construction for him, oh no! As far as he's concerned, it's cheating if your sukkah only takes ten minutes to put together.

No, it takes my better half hours of work and sweat, sometimes with the help of sons, neighbors, and the occasional immigrant laborer, to mount what must be the world's most extravagant low-budget sukkah. Our sukkah has hand-constructed and painted wooden panel walls, a wood floor, Moroccan hangings on the inner walls, a chandelier, "gilt" mirrors, and a bookshelf filled with prayer books and Gemaras. Last year he even got hold of an old breakfront somebody was giving away, gave it a coat of terra-cotta-colored paint, and hauled it into the sukkah, where he filled it with old family photos.

Our sukkah is so lavish that I joke that it's nicer than our house, and that we might as well move in year-round; our accountant frets that perhaps we need to start paying property taxes. It has even become something of a tourist attraction. Strangers have been known to peek their heads inside at odd hours, apologizing, "Oh, I didn't mean to intrude, but So-and-So told me I just *had* to come see your sukkah!"

Obviously, after all that effort, my family wants to spend the optimal amount of time "dwelling" in it, and they all start inviting people right and left to come for meals. The upshot is that I, as chief balabusta, spend rather more time dwelling in my kitchen and supermarket than the sukkah, as the food seems to disappear faster than I can cook it (this, of course, on the heels of the Rosh Hashanah and Yom Kippur meals, when I'm still panting with exhaustion from pulling off those *tours de force*). On the other hand, a good time really is had by all, as we enjoy our jewel box of a sukkah and spend happy hours around its table with good friends and good food.

The evenings of Sukkoth can range from hot and muggy to downright freezing, but most frequently are simply on the chilly side. This makes hot food like soups and stews especially appealing, as the guests dig in to literally warm their bellies. And since sitting in a sukkah on a crisp fall night is a perfect invitation for a hot bowl of soup, let me offer recipes for two tasty French soups that are not difficult to cook but make for an elegant presentation. The first, potato-leek soup, is similar to both Moroccan and Ashkenazi potato soups, but looks much more Parisian when stylishly dressed up with a fried-leek garnish I shamelessly copied from a soup I once enjoyed at a fancy wedding. The second, French onion soup, represents my attempt to create an authentic yet pareve version of this classic that surpasses the bland fare usually produced by soup mixes or even many restaurant kitchens.

French onion soup is traditionally topped with a slice of

toasted bread and cheese, and the whole thing is put under the broiler until the cheese is browned and melty. The traditional method presents two problems: a) every spoonful lifts up long strings of gloppy cheese that are nearly impossible to consume politely (*not* something to advise your marriage-age children to order on a first date), and b) not everyone has oven-proof soup bowls or a broiler they can use for dairy foods. So my solution is to pop a piece of bread with cheese on it into my dairy-only toaster oven, cut it into cubes once it's done, and throw them into the soup like croutons. Much easier to eat in public!

As we say in *francais, bon appetit!*

Potato-Leek Potage

2 tablespoons light olive oil or other cooking oil
2 leeks (well-cleaned, white part only)
1 onion
1 rib celery
4 cloves garlic. chopped coarsely
1 bay leaf
8 potatoes (peeled)
Salt, pepper
½ teaspoon thyme
Chicken broth or water mixed with two tablespoons chicken consommé powder

Garnish: Cut the first of the two leeks into short (1/2 inch) julienne sticks. Heat oil over medium-high heat and sauté leek pieces in oil until they begin to turn brown and caramelize around the edges (5-10 minutes). Remove from the oil with a slotted spoon and reserve.

Soup: Chop the remaining leek, the onion and the celery (I do this in a food processor). Reheat oil in the pot and sauté the vegetables until softened, adding the bay leaf and garlic. Chop the potatoes in a processor, add to the pot along with the spices and enough water so that the vegetables pieces are floating loosely in the broth. Simmer about 30 minutes; discard bay leaf and puree soup (an immersion blender is the most practical way to accomplish this). Ladle into bowls and garnish with a sprinkling of the reserved fried leeks.

French Onion Soup

2 tbsp light olive oil or cooking oil
4-5 onions, sliced into rings
1 tablespoon sugar
2 tablespoons cooking sherry
½ package onion soup mix (the packs that make a quart of soup) or about 3 tbsp onion powder
1 tablespoon pareve beef consommé powder
8 cups water
6 slices bread
6 slices mozzarella, gruyere, or other favorite cheese

Garnish: Top bread slices with cheese and toast until cheese is melted. Cut into one-inch cubes.

Soup: Heat oil over medium-high heat. Saute the onions until they begin to soften and become transparent; add sugar, stir, and continue sautéing until the onions are well browned and caramelized (this will take some time, about fifteen minutes). Add sherry, soup mixes, and salt and pepper to taste. Simmer 20 minutes. Serve topped with bread-and-cheese croutons.

P.S. A Note on the French and the Sephardim

The French have long believed themselves to represent the very summit of Western civilization, and among them are those who feel it is a sort of "French man's burden" to propagate the riches of French language and culture to the underprivileged foreign masses who know it not. In 1883, an organization called the Alliance Francaise was created for this very purpose, establishing schools in countries as far flung as Egypt, Syria, Iran and Vietnam.

But as the eternal question asks, what did this mean for the Jews? Jews living in Arab countries often found themselves within the range of a Jewish version, called Alliance Israelite. I regularly meet Sephardim from Arab countries such as Syria, Iran, and Egypt who tell me, "*Oui*, I learned to speak *francais* at the Alliance."

The exposure to French culture was probably a mixed blessing; on the one hand, it helped Jews acquire a language and education that propelled them into more sophisticated and higher-paying professions; on the other hand, on the spiritual level, Jews might have been better off foregoing an acquaintance with the very Torah-incompatible ideas of such French "luminaries" as Rousseau, Voltaire, and Balzac. More than a few Jewish souls left the fold for the French mainstream, blinded the first time they came face to face with the high dazzle of French elegance and style.

But, as we read in the "Aishet Chayil" (Woman of Valor) every Friday night, *shekker hachen v'hevel hayofi*—charm and beauty are deceiving. The lures of French culture can be at best skin-deep and at worst deceiving. The French colonization of Arab and African countries was often rapacious and cruel; after all, it was the French who gave us Robespierre, the Marquis de Sade and the guillotine. And on a culinary level, since that is what we are really here to talk about, who but the French could pull off that amazing coup of false advertising that managed to convince people that frogs' legs, snails, and cheese marbled with blue mold are the height of gourmet delicacy? Could these really be the same people who invented the baguette, the éclair, and quiche?

Today in France, many of the Sephardim from North Africa have become more French than the French themselves. Assimilation is rampant, as almost every family seems to have one member who married "out." But there is also a big movement towards greater observance, and more and more young people are beginning to search for meaning more profound than a well-crusted baguette and flawlessly tailored clothing. Many are leaving to settle in Israel, deeply disturbed by a growing Arab population that is not shy about harassing, beating up or even killing French Jews. "My family left Algeria to get away from hostile Arabs," one young woman told me. "But now the Arabs have followed us to France. What have we gained?"

But perhaps let's get back to happier topics; after all, Sukkoth is called *zeman simchateinu*, the time of our rejoicing. We dwell in our sukkahs in order to remind ourselves that no matter where we Jews build our homes, ultimately God is the only One who protects us. Let's go cook some soup and enjoy our sukkahs wherever they happen to be.

Chapter 12

Nuts About Doughnuts!

WHEN THE FLEDGLING state of Israel first began rebranding itself for the outside world, those in charge of PR decided it was high time to put a new spin on the old Jewish stereotypes. Begone the stooped, malnourished ghetto dweller, shivering from the bitter winters of eastern Europe, with barely enough strength to hoist his tome of Talmud! This miserable *shlemiel* would now be replaced by hardy, muscle-bound farmers and soldiers bronzed by the blazing sun of the Middle East. To nourish these new UberJews, new "Jewish" foods were "invented," like falafel and hummus. And let's get it straight about Chanukah, folks: people in the new Israel don't do latkes anymore, like those potato-eating, European-born Jews: they eat *soufganiyot*, or doughnuts. How exotic!

Of course, the truth is that Jews from Arab countries *never* had a custom to eat potato latkes (potatoes, by the way, were a late arrival even in Europe, having been brought to Spain from the New World in 1565). Sephardim celebrated the Chanukah custom to eat food fried in oil by making fried cakes. We know that Jews were eating fried cakes at least as far back as the time of Maimonides, since he specifically writes that--ahem--too much fried bread or cake is not good for the health!

But try telling that to Jews at Chanukah time, when the men bring home extra bakery doughnuts from shul in the morning for breakfast and then sit down in the evening equally inspired to put away the homemade version! And the kids are treated to them in school as well! My husband still has fond memories of coming out of the Jewish high school he attended in Casablanca to find the "doughnut man" at his stand on the corner, expertly pulling off balls of dough, poking a finger through the middle to make the hole, then throwing them into the oil.

One of the joys and burdens of being in a "mixed" marriage is that I end up trying to accommodate the favorite *minhagim,* or customs, for both of us, which often makes for double the work, not to mention double the calories. For example, I do hamantaschen on Purim as well as traditional Moroccan rolls with an egg in the center, and on Chanukah we make latkes *and* doughnuts. But I've enjoyed taking on the doughnut tradition; there is something wonderfully cozy about lighting the menorah on a snowy winter night and sitting down to a pot of hot mint tea and a platter of doughnuts just out of the frying pan. We sprinkle them with confectioner's sugar and put out jars of honey and jam for everyone to take their pick. The Moroccans call their doughnuts *sfeng* (although those who prefer to sound European call them by the French name *beignets*). The Jews from Spanish-speaking roots call them *birmuelos* (with the distinction that a traditional *birmuelo* has no hole), and the Tunisians make a cake-like doughnut called a yoyo.

Perhaps the best *sfeng* I have ever had were made during the week of my niece's wedding in Israel. One of her family's Moroccan neighbors brought over a platter of *sfeng* that were like something out of Donut Utopia—light, tender, not at all oily. Since then I have looked through cookbook after cookbook trying to find out what made the crucial difference in Tzippo-rah's doughnuts, but every *sfeng* recipe I find is more or less the same: flour, water, salt, yeast, perhaps a little sugar. So what *was* it? Perhaps the Israeli flour? Like the Lost Chord, I am still searching for that Lost Doughnut, and every year I try to approximate it a little better.

In the meantime, my own *sfeng* are a reasonably close second, and they always contribute to creating a "Chappy Chanukah."

Moroccan *Sfeng*

2 packages dry yeast (about 4 ½ teaspoons)
1 tablespoon sugar
3 cups warm water
1 teaspoon salt
7 cups all-purpose flour
Vegetable oil for frying

Dissolve yeast and sugar in the water in a large bowl. When yeast begins to foam, add the salt and flour and knead gently to form a very light, soft dough. (If dough is too wet, add more flour; if too dry, add a little more water.) Cover and let rise for two hours.

Without punching down the dough, pull off small balls of dough, make a generous hole in the center (the surrounding dough will rise and fill in fast during frying). Let the donuts rise on baking sheets another 20-30 minutes, until puffy. Heat two inches of oil in a large frying pan (to about 375 degrees--you can use a candy thermometer to check) and fry in the hot oil (turn doughnuts over when bottom becomes golden). Drain on paper towels; dust with confectioner's sugar and serve with assorted jams and honey.

Tunisian Yoyos

4 large eggs

1/4 cup sugar

1 tablespoon oil

4 1/2 cups all-purpose flour

2 teaspoons baking powder

2 teaspoons vanilla sugar

1 teaspoon orange-blossom water (optional)

1 teaspoon grated orange zest

Oil for frying

Syrup:

1 cup sugar

2 cups water

2 tbsp lemon Juice

1 cup honey

Beat together eggs, sugar and one tablespoon oil in a medium bowl with an electric mixer until creamy. In a large bowl, mix flour and baking powder. Fold egg batter into flour with a spoon. Add vanilla sugar, orange water and orange zest. Combine ingredients until the mixture is slightly sticky. (If it is too sticky add more flour, if too dry add a little oil.) Turn the dough out onto a floured board and knead for a few minutes. Form into a large ball and cover with a clean towel; let rest 30 minutes.

Roll dough into small balls and make a hole in the middle, let rise 20 minutes. Pour two inches of oil into a deep frying pan and heat to about 375 degrees. Fry the yoyos until golden, turning once. Remove and drain on paper towel.

Shortly before you are ready to cook the doughnuts, make the syrup by placing the sugar, water, and lemon juice in a saucepan. Bring to the boil, stirring, and cook until the sugar dissolves. Reduce the heat, then stir in the honey and simmer for 10 minutes. Keep warm. Dip the yoyos into honey syrup and serve immediately.

Chapter 13

A Bejeweled Persian Tu B'Shvat

I ONCE LEARNED IN A SHIUR, or Torah lecture, that the Hebrew word for man, Adam, contains the same letters as *m'od*, meaning very much or very. The reason for this, the speaker explained, is that it is human nature to always want to do *very much*; we're never satisfied with the status quo. Translated into balabusta terms, this means: why make one kugel for Shabbos when you can make two? And if you still have half an hour left to play with, why not make three?

Some people are better than others at realistically recognizing their limitations; I am not one of them. I may kvetch a lot, but in fact I often do enjoy a challenge (you know, like when five people call for a Shabbos invitation at 2:00 on a winter Friday when sundown is at 4:30, initiating a mad rush to add more potatoes to the stew and throw together an extra dessert). So when my husband brought home a Sephardi custom to eat fifteen fruits on Tu B'Shvat, the holidays honoring the new year for the trees,I took this as a challenge too, racking my brain how to incorporate fifteen fruits into one festive meal. I thought it might be hard; as it turned out, I ended up with over twenty!

"Are you crazy?" was the reaction of an Ashkenazic friend of mine. "In my house we just eat a little carob to mark the holiday, and that's it. And my kids get *peckalach* [little bags] of dried fruit in school, but they never eat it. I'm the one who ends up finishing the bag. . .what should I do, throw it in the garbage?"

But Tu B'Shvat deserves more honor than that, and it's not hard, if you're cooking Sephardi style, to include a lot of fruits and nuts; olives also count as a fruit. Meats and poultry are often stewed with fruits, and meals are typically ended with a bowl of fruit and some nuts and/or seeds. Even the rice may include fruit and/or nuts.

Which brings me to one of the most memorable rice dishes I ever tasted, a Persian classic combining basmati rice, fruits and nuts known as "jeweled rice." I first sampled it at a bat mitzvah dinner that was held in an elegant Persian restaurant in Long Island. Talk about a Jewish melting pot: the bat mitzvah girl was the daughter of a Mexican-Syrian mother and a Moroccan-Yemenite-Israeli father, and how did they celebrate? With Persian food! Go figure!

At any rate, the jeweled rice truly was memorable, flecked with bits of candied orange peel and dried fruits and nuts. All by itself, it probably contained at least ten different ingredients that qualify for the *ha'etz* blessing, the blessing made before eating fruits that come from a tree. It was delicately perfumed with exotic spices and was a beautiful orange color. A little research turned up that this royal dish is traditionally served at weddings (and maybe the occasional bat mitzvah?). I decided I had to learn how it was done.

Jeweled rice is made with basmati rice, which many cooks

rinse through several changes of water before cooking so that it doesn't cook up sticky from rice dust. It also incorporates saffron threads steeped in hot water, which give an exotic perfume, but since saffron is expensive and sometimes difficult to find, you could substitute a quarter teaspoon of tumeric in the cooking water. One authentic-looking recipe I found calls for dried rose-buds and green cardamom pods, but since these are also not easily available in your average corner grocery you could omit them without the dish suffering too much; the same recipe called for a berry I'd never heard of called barberries, which are apparently small, tart berries (dried cranberries will have to serve as a plausible substitute). The most labor-intensive part of the recipe is making the candied orange peel and carrot strips, but don't omit that step: it's what gives the rice its "jeweled" look and flavor.

But what to serve it with? Persian cuisine is ancient and venerable, and many of its recipes call for stewing meat with fruit. I called my friend Dalia, who grew up in the Persian town of Shiraz and was smuggled with her sister, terrified, out of Iran on the back of a truck in the late 1980's. She suggested a recipe for meat with quinces, which is also perfect for Tu B'Shvat because most of us don't buy quinces on a regular basis (if ever), which would qualify us to be able to actually make a *shechiyanu* blessing (the blessing over enjoying something new) upon eating them. (In case you never had occasion to "meet a handsome quince," as it were, quinces are a hard yellow-green fruit that look and taste much like a very sour apple, the main difference being that they cost four times as much.) "But this dish takes awhile to cook," Dalia warned me. "There is no such thing as fast food in Persian cooking!"

But Dalia's recipe, while requiring substantial simmering time, is not difficult to prepare, and it can simmer while you *potchke* with the jeweled rice. Between the five ingredients in the rice and two more in the meat, you have seven fruits already for a fifteen-fruit feast. Now just add some olives, dates, figs, and carob from the Holy Land, plus a bowl of other fruits and nuts or a tart topped with several types of sliced fruit, and you have a meal that will give Tu B'Shvat all the honor it deserves!

Persian Jeweled Rice (*Javaher Polow*)

¼ tsp. saffron or ¼ tsp turmeric, dissolved in 2 cups boiling water
1 cup basmati rice, rinsed several times until water runs clear
1 teaspoon salt
1 teaspoon cinnamon
½ teaspoon cumin
½ cup sugar
Peel of one orange (see below)
½ carrot
2 tablespoon margarine
¼ cup dried cranberries
¼ cup golden raisins
½ cup chopped roasted almonds (or ¼ cup chopped almonds and ¼ cup chopped roasted pistachios)
1 onion
About 2 teaspooons oil

Use a vegetable peeler to peel long strips of peel off the orange, avoiding the pith (reserve orange for another use). Chop strips into small pieces (a diamond shape is decorative). Now use the peeler to peel long strips from the carrot half. Boil the ½ cup water with ½ cup sugar into a syrup, add the orange bits and carrot strips and boil for ten minutes (not too much longer or the mixture will start to harden and become candy). Drain orange and carrot bits and set aside.

Put the two cups saffron water along with four more cups

of water into a large saucepan and bring to a boil. Add the rinsed basmati rice, salt, cinnamon, and cumin and boil ten minutes. Drain the rice in a colander. Now melt the margarine in the same saucepan and add the rice back in, mixing it with the candied orange peel and carrot strips. Turn off the burner.

In a small saucepan, sauté the onion in a little oil until well browned. While this is sautéing, soak the raisins and cranberries in hot water for ten minutes, then drain the water. Combine with the sautéed onions.

To serve, mound the rice on a large platter and top with the onions, cranberries and raisins; garnish with the chopped nuts. Serves about eight. Fit for a king!

Dalia's Meat With Quinces and Prunes

2 tablespoons oil
2 large onions
2 pounds beef stew meat
4 plum tomatoes, chopped
1 teaspoon turmeric
1 tablespoon paprika
Salt, pepper
1 ½ cups pitted prunes (real Persians use sour prunes, if you can find them)
2 quinces, peeled, cut into small chunks
Juice of one lemon (optional)

Saute onions in the oil over medium high heat until transparent. Add the meat and brown it, then add the tomatoes and sauté a few minutes more. Add water to cover, bring to a boil and then simmer one hour, partially covered, or until tender. Add prunes, quinces and lemon juice if desired and stew another half hour, until the water is mostly evaporated and has cooked down into a sauce. Serves 8-10.

Chapter 14

Cooking Up Fun for Purim

What's in a Jewish name? Sometimes you can find traces of the family's history. Take my own family's name, Bensoussan: It's a Moroccan distortion of the Hebrew Ben–Shushan, which means "son of Shushan." Shushan, for those in the know, is none other than the Persian *Shushan ha-birah*, the capital city of Achashveiros' 127 provinces, where the story of Purim took place. When you have a name like Ben-shushan, you feel a special connection to Purim—and to "Shushan Purim," the day after Purim, all the more!

So we Ben-Shushans have always felt a certain obligation to do Purim up in a big way, inviting lots of people to our *seudah* and preparing large quantities of *mishloach manot*, the gift packages of food that are traditionally distributed to friends. Some years ago, when I had more energy and less brains, I would prepare elaborate packages to give away, taking seriously the concept that *mishloach manot* should consist of real food (as opposed to Laffy Taffy, lollipops, and Fruit-by-the-Foot). One year, for example, possessed by who-knows-what foolhardy inspiration, I decided to give out an assortment of homemade Sephardic cooked salads—my varicose veins still remember the countless hours on my feet preparing that one. It was eagerly devoured by the balabustas but ignored by all the kids—who are, of course, unmoved by anything that doesn't promise to create a sugar high, produce diabetes, and/or put the dentist's kids through college.

I also learned the hard way that it may not pay to knock oneself out making homemade challah rolls or hamantaschen for distribution. Even if yours are outstandingly delicious, Purim is such a hectic day that chances are they will end up mixed together with all the rest in one big pile by the evening and you won't get a single call from a neighbor to compliment you on your hard work and culinary prowess.

For the balabusta, the bad news is that Purim means preparing, in addition to all the *mishloach manot*, three family meals: something to break the fast the first night, something to eat in the morning after hearing the *megillah*, and the *seudah*. (The good news: with all those *mishloach manos* packages, chances are you won't have to worry about making dessert!) In my home, planning the morning meal is a no-brainer; Moroccans have a custom to eat Israeli-style couscous cooked with milk, called *berkoks*, after shul. Spiked with cinnamon and sugar, it's like eating a bowl of hot cereal. That coupled with a few bagels or goodies from the *mishloach manot* usually tides everyone over till the *seudah*.

Later, for the *seudah*, we often serve a regular couscous with lamb or beef stew. As this meal is rather the last hurrah before Pesach, I consider it an opportunity to use up all the frozen boureka dough and filo dough in the freezer to make hors d'oeuvres like cigares, pastels and bourekas. There's also a custom to bake challah with hard-boiled eggs in the center, which are considered the eyes of Haman, the wicked villain of the Purim story. The kids gleefully gouge out the eyes, or at least break the shells and eat the eggs.

In many ways Purim festivities remind me of a wedding, and not just because all the little girls are decked out in white sateen "kallah" dresses. Like a wedding, it involves spending a lot of time finding the right clothes/costumes for the family; it means planning a *seudah* that your family and friends attend together, complete with libations, singing and dancing, and the giving and receiving of presents. Like a wedding, the whole thing takes a tremendous amount of energy and preparation and yet goes by in a tornado of activity and goodwill before you know it. In fact, by the end of the day you'd swear a tornado actually did barrel through the house, what with all those candy wrappers and confetti and hamantaschen crumbs scattered across the floor, and the whole family sitting around looking completely shell-shocked.

But nobody is allowed to loll around with glazed eyes for too long, because the end of Purim means. . .Pesach is coming! Goodbye to drunken revelry, and hello to hard work and slavery! Oh well, that's one way to work off all those calories before we start stuffing ourselves at the next holiday table. . .

Purim Rolls

Challah dough (I double my challah recipe, so figure enough dough for two large challahs)
1 dozen eggs, hardboiled
1 raw egg, beaten, for glazing

Once the dough has risen (preferably twice), divide it into twelve portions. Take about ¼ of a portion and divide in two. Roll the two portions into two ropes about six inches long. Roll the remaining dough into a ball, flatten it a little and make a hollow in the center, and put the egg inside. Now take the two dough ropes and criss-cross them over the egg, securing the ends under the roll. (I score the lower rope with a knife in the center, where the other rope will cross it, to make a little trough for it to rest in. It prevents the X shape from sliding while baking.) Brush the dough with the beaten egg and bake for about half an hour at 350 degrees.

Berkoks

½ pound acini pepe pasta or untoasted Israeli couscous
¼ teaspoon salt
3 cups milk
1 teaspoon cinnamon
White or brown sugar

Bring a large pot of water to boil. Add salt and pasta, stirring. Cook until pasta is *al dente* (softened but still resists the bite) about ten minutes.

Drain the pasta of almost all the water (does not have to be completely drained). Add milk and cinnamon and bring the mixture to a simmer. Simmer several minutes (keep an eye on the pot so the milk doesn't scorch; if necessary, add more water or milk). Ladle into bowls and add sugar to taste.

Lamb Tagine With Couscous

You can make the couscous the authentic way, as given in the recipe, or simply prepare it according to package directions. Personally, I find that packages instructing you to dump couscous in boiling water and fluff after five minutes give you a couscous that is either dry or gluey, but certainly not the fluffy, moist, separate grains that come from cooking it the "real" way. If you must do "instant" couscous, in my experience the packages that give microwave instructions produce the best results.

2 tablespoons olive oil

3 pounds lamb stew or lamb shoulder cut in 1-1/2-inch cubes

3 large onions, cut in eighths

2 cloves garlic, coarsely chopped

1 teaspoon cinnamon

1 teaspoon turmeric

Salt, pepper

Chicken broth (may make with hot water and consommé powder), about 3 cups

5 large carrots, cut in chunks

1 small butternut squash, peeled, seeded and cut into chunks

1 zucchini, peeled and cut in 1-inch rounds

1 15-ounce can chickpeas, rinsed and drained

1 ½ cups pitted prunes

8 ounces couscous plus 1 tablespoon oil

1/3 cup toasted sliced almonds

In a large pot or couscoussier, brown the onions in the oil over medium high heat, until starting to brown around the edges, about ten minutes. Add the garlic and lamb chunks and brown the meat on each side. Add the spices and chicken broth to cover the meat; bring to a boil, then turn the flame down and simmer, partially covered, for an hour and fifteen minutes, until meat begins to soften.

In the meantime, rinse the couscous in water in a pan. Drain off almost all of the water and add a tablespoon of oil; mix well and let stand for half an hour. Now line a colander or strainer with cheesecloth (or use the top half of the couscoussier), and place on top of the bubbling meat, covered tightly, until the meat has softened, about another half hour.

Stir the couscous with a fork to distribute the moisture. Cover again after adding the vegetables, prunes, and chickpeas to the meat. Simmer the entire thing another twenty minutes, until the vegetables are soft.

To serve, mound the couscous on a large serving platter and garnish with some of the vegetables and almonds. Transfer the meat and the rest of the vegetables to another platter, top with almonds, and serve alongside.

Chapter 15

Pass on Passover? Not On Your Life!

FOR MOST OF the latter half of my brilliant public elementary school career in Levittown, PA, Alan Schwartz and I were always the only Jewish kids in our class. He always had the most stars on the math quiz chart and I always had the most stars on the spelling quiz chart, and between all these important distinctions we found ourselves set apart and thrown together quite a bit.

Alan's family was Conservative; mine, at the time, was unaffiliated except for a Workman's Circle group, which meant that for a few years I got sent with a small group of girls to learn Yiddish from a little old man in the basement of a bank. The little old man spent as much time in the bathroom "washing his hands" as he did teaching us aleph-bais and simple conversation. But the Workman's Circle group always got together for holiday celebrations and at least made sure the kids knew the difference between *Maoz Tzur* and *Mah Nishtanah*.

I vividly remember sitting next to Alan in the school cafeteria at Pesach time, opening up our brown paper bags to find we had more or less the same lunch: boiled chicken, hard-boiled eggs, matzoh and macaroons from the can. "Gee, does your family keep kosher all the time, or only on Pesach?" Alan asked conversationally. I was nine years old and had no idea what he meant. I figured he must be referring to throwing out all the bread in the house, which we did observe faithfully. But of course I was too embarrassed to ask for clarification. "Only on Pesach," I said with more certainty than I felt. At least the crunch of my matzoh was emphatic. "Yeah, mine keeps kosher for Pesach too," Alan concurred, unwrapping a cellophane-covered leg of boiled chicken.

Today, over thirty years have passed since that conversation. My family moved away from Levittown and Alan Schwartz, and my education continued in other places: high school, college, a stint in Jerusalem in seminary and a lot of other Jewish learning far beyond what the hand-washing old man ever taught us. The result of all this is that today I am finally in a position to give Alan Schwartz an unqualified answer to his question. Today, friends, I could answer Alan Schwartz in no uncertain terms:

"*Yes,* Alan, yes! We *do* keep kosher all year long!-- and for Pesach too!--Oh *boy,* do we keep kosher!"

For now that I have become Jewishly Enlightened, I have learned that I need to start getting nervous as soon as we hit Rosh Chodesh Adar. Fear and Trembling set in as I realize that from there it's only two short weeks to get my act together for Purim, which in my family is always a big rollicking affair. Then, once the last *mishloach manot* is given out and the stray couscous and crushed lollipops vacuumed off the dining room floor, my ears start to ring with the ticking of the Pesach count-down clock. In Manhattan they count down the minutes on New Year's Eve, in Times Square, but in Brooklyn we start counting down minutes on Shushan Purim...waiting for the matzoh ball to drop?!

.Of course matters are never helped when I run into my neighbor who remarks breezily, "Oh, I started cleaning at Chanukah time, and anyway in my family nobody *ever* brings food into the bedrooms or the basement..." My heart sinks. I do my best to dismiss her in my mind as a clearly deranged obsessive-compulsive. Underneath, of course, I'm really just jealous: jealous that a) she's clearly better organized than me, b) she now has much less work ahead of her than me, and c) she is clearly a better parent than me if she has successfully managed to discipline her toddlers never to trail cookies beyond the kitchen door and her teenagers never to sneak bags of chips into their rooms.

After all those strenuous hours spent making and unmaking Purim, though, I'm simply too wiped out to start cleaning for Pesach right away. But I'd feel too guilty indulging in a few free hours for myself when the idea YOU SHOULD BE STARTING FOR PESACH looms over my head, a storm cloud just waiting to rain all over my parade. So I do what any self-respecting Jewish Princess does when she's down and depressed: I go shopping! All the kids need new outfits for Pesach, right? And you have to start early to find just what you need, especially for young ladies who have strong opinions about what's acceptable or not among the jury of their peers. So I hit the stores, congratulating myself on having found a great excuse to both spend gobs of money and avoid housework at the same time.

But once having hit my credit limit and run out of excuses and ways to procrastinate, it's time to face reality. I sigh, roll up my sleeves and attack the house. And then—oh miracle of miracles! I find that I actually get into it! I *like* reorganizing, throwing out, turning up lost socks and earrings, purging the entire family from the excess consumption of an entire year. I like vacuuming dust from places I didn't know were dusty. The change is most radical in the kitchen, as I banish the crumbs in the shelves, the half-finished package of noodles, the leftover bottle of beer from Purim, the "mistakes" like that bottle of lemon extract I bought for a recipe and never touched again. The freezer itself is a foray into high adventure as it yields forth a steady stream of UFO's (Unidentified Frozen Objects).

If cleanliness is next to G-dliness, then G-d is surely very close at Pesach time. (*This* is called spirituality? I groan as I scrub grease off the oven door.) As we clean and scrub we make our *mikdash me'at,* our own domestic sanctuaries, that much more new and shiny, a more fitting place for Him to dwell. We go through our possessions and hopefully feel gratitude that we have so many of them, unlike generations past where even a shoestring would have been saved and reused instead of cavalierly tossed into the garbage. We imitate Hashem in our own small ways as we make order out of chaos, as we take the raw stuff of our lives and try to renew it and make it more attractive. Although we work like slaves, we do so with the goal of feeling like kings in our castles once Pesach finally arrives.

Pesach is a lesson in overcoming complacency, in learning that we can always do more than we think we can. How many times have I gone to bed leaving dishes in the sink because I protest I'm simply too bushed to tackle them? But *erev* Pesach the dishes get done, and much, much more each day, until the muscles groan in protest. In pushing ourselves to the limits, we discover that we're stronger than we thought we were, more efficient, able to make every minute count. It comes with single-minded dedication to a goal: GET THE HOUSE READY FOR PESACH. Imagine what we could accomplish if we attacked every goal with the same singleness of purpose and eye on the calendar!

And then, finally, the house is done. The kitchen gleams like a laboratory, with freshly lined shelves and a fridge that would lead the ignorant outsider to assume we'd just bought half the stock in the Reynolds aluminum company. I can't even bear the thought of messing it up by starting to cook. "Can't we..." I quaver, "Can't we just... *look* at it for awhile?"

Not only does it look unnaturally clean, it looks so *empty!* The spice cabinet, normally bursting with every spice Ashkenazi, Sephardi, Chinese and Indian, now barely contains a box of salt and a few lonely containers of pepper, cinammon and paprika. Banished the five-spice powder I bought and used exactly once for some weird Chinese recipe, gone the za'atar and chili powder and blue food coloring for that birthday cake last November. There are less dishes in the cabinets—no excess weight here either. Banished with the *chametz* are the heart-shaped muffin pan I bought to support some charity and the tart pans in four sizes. I feel so purified, so stripped down of unessentials—why, I feel light as a matzoh ball!

I also have to admit I get a certain perverse satisfaction out of seeing my kids deprived of most of their usual junky snacks. Oh, there are kosher l'Pesach junk foods available (more and more each year, I'm afraid), but in the first place, they're expensive, and in the second place my family tries to avoid a lot of processed food during Pesach. So my kids find themselves actually obliged to snack on... *fruit!* Oh brave new world! During the year the bad tended to drive out the good, but now that those cookies and pretzels have disappeared they discover, to their great surprise, just how good an apple or orange can taste.

And you know what? Despite the limited range of ingredients, despite the absence of a large variety of spices, *all* the food tastes wonderful: fresh, springlike, simple. How refreshing it is to live more simply! To have a narrower range of choices instead of twenty kinds of breakfast cereal and thirty kinds of chips! Not so very long ago people struggled hard just to have the minimum they needed to subsist. Today, we are so inundated by products and goods that we have a completely different challenge: to learn to limit ourselves within a sea of material wealth. We need to learn to "just say no," to take what we need and not consume in excess: to limit the quantities we eat, the quantities of clothing we buy or accept from friends and family, to tone down the extravagance of family celebrations like weddings and bar mitzvahs.

Learning to live joyfully within material limits is actually a lesson we were supposed to have absorbed earlier in the year, at Succoth time, when we left our comfortable homes and lived in our makeshift "booths" for a week. We sat happily surrounded by a few flimsy walls, eating off folding tables, feasting and singing and having the time of our lives. The lesson here is that when we are well infused with spirituality and inner joy, we can live quite happily with lower standards of material comfort. And the converse holds true as well: it is when we are spiritually empty and unhappy that we run hard to plug the void with an overabundance of possessions and entertainment.

And so we launch ourselves into the celestial realm of Planet Pesach, going on a vacation of sorts without ever leaving home. As a wise person once said, a change is as good as a rest, and our lives change within the very four walls of our homes. The children's eyes shine as they sit at the Seder table, seeing their home transformed and their parents presiding like royalty. The food is different and special. We don't go to school or pay bills or go to work; we dress more nicely than usual; we enjoy hours of family time together doing fun things we don't usually make the time to do.

And then, before we know it, it's all over. The Pesach dishes get whisked into cartons and my husband runs out to buy flour and yeast for *mimouna*, the Moroccan post-Pesach celebration. All too quickly life becomes busy and cluttered again; as I put my regular pots back on the shelves I marvel at how *dirty* they look compared to the gleaming, once-a-year pots I have for Pesach. We bring up boxes and boxes and more boxes...where did all this stuff *come* from? I groan as I unpack the blue food coloring.

I think of the people who say, "Can't wait for Mashiach to come; they say once he comes we won't have to make Pesach any more!" And then I think of all those people who just throw in the towel and go down to hotels, shelling out a bundle to spend an entertaining but dubiously meaningful Pesach in Disneyland or Sedona.

What, stop making Pesach and miss out on all the fun? Why, I wouldn't miss it for the world!

Never Out-"Dated" for Pesach: Sephardic Haroseth

Every year when my birthday rolls around and the kids want to know how old I am, they get the same frustrating answer: "Twenty-nine going on twenty-nine." Of course, by now even the most mathematically challenged of my kids has figured out there is something fishy about this response; after all, if my oldest is already twenty, chances are I didn't give birth to her at the tender age of nine.

But even if fortysomething is the new thirtysomething, it is still quite clear that I'm from the old (read: fuddy-duddy) generation, that pitiful generation that grew up deprived of iPads and cell phones and still remains woefully uninitiated into the mysteries of TikTok and ChatGPT. When I was a kid, I tell them, we had big, bulky stereos the size of a dresser instead of sleek devices that fit into your pocket; we had computers that took up entire rooms instead of one side of your briefcase. And in my best *When Zeide Was Young* voice I also inform them that when *I* was a kid, Pesach actually meant. . .DOING WITHOUT!

103

Have you *seen* the Pesach aisles of recent years? Since there is always the minute possibility that one of us, Heaven forefend, might develop severe withdrawal symptoms due to an entire week of cold-turkey *chametz* deprivation, we now have everything from kosher-for-Pesach noodles to kosher–for–Pesach bagels to kosher l'Pesach pizza! We have cereal, croutons, ice cream, candy bars! ("It's for the kids," the people say with a shrug, as they throw another box of Pesach-compliant imitation Cheerios into their carts.) The contemporary combination of merchandisers eager to make money and consumers loathe to give up their favorite indulgences for one fleeting week has created an explosion of Pesach offerings.

But those of us in the 'old-fuddy-duddy' category still remember the hungry years, the Olden Days when "Pesach treat" meant a hunk of bittersweet chocolate bark or jellied, sugared "fruit slices" in traffic-light shades of green, yellow and red. Or—perish the thought—a piece of fruit. I still remember my grandmother, *a"h*, urging a cardboard box of dates on us kids, trying to persuade us: "It's better than candy!" *Better than candy?* I thought with deep, nine-year-old skepticism. *Says who?* Of course, this was the same grandmother who would offer us glasses of "cherry soda," meaning she would plop a hefty dollop of her homemade cherry preserves into seltzer water and swish it around till it blended. (That didn't fool us either, not for a minute, even though the taste was surprisingly good.)

But now that my tastes have grown up considerably, I have to admit that Grandma was probably right: dates really *are* better than candy (but maybe not chocolate). Where my husband comes from, in those exotic Arab lands of swaying palms and spitting camels, dates were a staple for snacks and desserts. And this was even more the case on Pesach, when pastries were not an option.

Dates are the basis for most Sephardic versions of *haroseth*, that fruit and nut concoction used during the Seder to symbolize the mortar the enslaved Jews used to make bricks for the Egyptians. Dates make a thicker, pastier haroseth than the Ashkenazic mix of chopped apples and nuts (which I have also adored since childhood). I make my haroseth with dates, raisins, nuts, wine, and some cinnamon and ginger; it's so yummy that I have to make extra to serve as a spread throughout the entire holiday. The Syrians stew dates for haroseth until they are soupy, then reconstitute them with nuts; I have seen Italian recipes for haroseth that include dates and bananas, Turkish recipes with dates and oranges, Persian recipes calling for dates and pomegranate seeds, and Yemenite recipes that contain dates and hot pepper (apparently the Yemenite position is: If it ain't spicy, it just ain't *food*!)

My *consuegra,* as one says in Ladino, or in Yiddish *machetainesta* (English: my child-in-law's mother) tells me that the Syrians traditionally stuff dates with nuts and serve them as a Pesach dessert. This makes perfect sense, since Syrians are into stuffing food to about the same extent Yemenites are into hot spices. Syrian cuisine includes about a zillion varieties of *mechshi*, or stuffed vegetables, which are always a presence at Pesach time ("If it's a vegetable, we stuff it," one Syrian friend tells me). And since *mechshi* is delicious, the temptation is to eat it until you are similarly. . .stuffed!

But—to get back to dates—they really are the perfect natural "candy" for Pesach. If you haven't ever tried those fat, moist Medjool dates then you haven't really eaten dates; the little California ones don't come close in texture or flavor. One word of caution to the kosher gastronome: dates should be opened and checked for worms before consumption, since worms enjoy a yummy date as much as you and I do. And on the nutritional side, since dates are praised as an aid to digestion, perhaps the Sephardim are on to something: it's not a bad idea to serve them at the close of the meal, after we've all ingested our halachic measure of matzoh and so much, much more. . .

On that cheerful and healthy note, I will close by offering some date-based haroseth recipes and a recipe for stuffed dates, which are sure to contribute to a happy and kosher Passover!

North African haroseth
1 pound dates
½ cup raisins
½ cup sweet wine
1 teaspoon cinnamon
½ teaspoon ginger or a small piece of fresh ginger
½ cup walnuts

Grind ingredients together in a food processor, adding a little more wine if mixture is too thick to blend.

Yemenite haroseth
This is from an Israeli cookbook by Hava Nathan.
1 pound dates
1 pound raisins
3 whole pomegranates, peeled and seeded
¾ pound almonds
½ pound walnuts
1 tablespoon mixed ground spices: cinnamon, hot paprika, cumin, cardamom, cloves and ginger

Chop all ingredients together by hand or in a processor, adding spices to taste.

Venetian Haroseth

1 pound dates
1 pounds figs
1 large ripe banana
2 tablespoons poppy seeds
1 cup chopped nuts (walnuts, almonds or a combination)
½ cup pine nuts
Zest of one orange
½ cup sultana raisins
¼ cup dried apricots
½ cup brandy
Honey

Chop all ingredients together in a processor, using the brandy and honey to bind it.

Syrian Stuffed Dates

There are fancier versions of this recipe that require stuffing the dates with a paste of almonds and sugar, and/or making a syrup to spoon over the them, but these are delicious enough as they are —and who needs extra fuss at Pesach time?

24 Medjool dates (can substitute pitted prunes)
24 walnut halves or whole blanched almonds
Sugar (regular granulated or powdered)

Open each date, stuff it with a nut, close it back up and roll it in sugar.

Chapter 16

Memories of Mimouna

MIMOUNA, for those not in the know, is a traditional Moroccan party held the night Pesach ends, in which large, flat, yeasted pancakes called *mofleta* are always served.

My sister-in-law tells it like something out of the Arabian Nights. "My father-in-law was the president of the Jewish community of Marakech," she says, "so he used to host a *mimouna* for the entire community at his home. The maids knew that as soon as the last meal of the chag was over, it was their signal to begin boxing up the Pesach dishes, and as soon as the holiday was over they would finish changing the kitchen back and begin preparing for the party. Of course, for the party itself they'd hire extra help in the kitchen."

Cases of liquor would be delivered, along with bags of flour and yeast; an Oriental orchestra would come and set up. As my sister-in-law speaks I imagine a large villa, painted in the burnt-pumpkin and umber tones of Marrakech, surrounded by a high wall and guarded by an Arab in a djellaba. I hear the bustle in the kitchen and high laughter as the mistress of the house works alongside her maids, feverishly coaxing oiled balls of dough into mofleta, which come out of the frying pan looking something like a cross between a matzoh and a pancake. The party starts: I imagine women flitting, butterfly-like, through the rooms in their brightly colored, embroidered silk caftans, and the men wearing djellabas and pouring whiskey over the ice in their glasses. Limousines arrive bearing not only Jewish leaders but Arab and French dignitaries as well; at times somebody will take the mike from the band leader to make a little speech or sing a popular Arabic favorite with the musicians.

The grandiose *mimouna* parties of Morocco's belle époque are largely a thing of the past, except perhaps among the wealthy few remaining in Casablanca or the Moroccan stronghold of Montreal. But nobody is willing to give up the tradition altogether. Man people these days make smaller parties in the homes, or in a shul. We once arrived at one of the Moroccan shuls in Brooklyn, only to find four balabustas frantically trying to produce enough mofleta for a crowd using four improvised hot plates, as the guests waited impatiently for seconds. It's a lot harder when you don't have a small army of servants at your disposition to smooth things along.

In my house we have our own humble routine more or less established. Everybody pitches in right after *havdalah* to box up the Pesach dishes, while my husband runs out to Shop Rite for flour and yeast. I keep a box of dairy frying pans and utensils marked with the *hametz* dishes so I know where to find them right away. On the occasions when my mother-in-law is with us for the holiday, she always insists that I be the first to plunge my hand into the bowl of flour, yeast and water to begin kneading, explaining superstitiously that she's a widow and isn't allowed to initiate the process.

Maybe it's the smell wafting through the open windows into the spring night air, but people always seem to be magnetically pulled to the house for a few *mofleta*, eaten slathered with butter, honey and jam. Our Israeli, Sephardic-but-not-Moroccan neighbors always make pizza, which they gaily send over in exchange for a platter of our mofleta.

Moroccans are a stubborn bunch amidst a stubborn-and-stiff-necked people, and they will not relinquish their *mimouna* any time soon even though most are no longer in their country of origin. At the very least, everybody wants to eat *mofleta*; it is a taste acquired in childhood that is not easily relinquished, in the same way we look forward to hamantaschen on Purim or raisin challah on Rosh Hashanah.

Food is never just food. It's memory, it's tradition, it's mother love. I saw this illustrated some years ago when I did a stint as an ESL teacher with elderly Russian Jews. Seventy years of Communism had all but wiped out most of their Jewish knowledge—they were vague about Sukkot, had never heard of Tu B'Shvat or Tisha B'Av and confused the names hopelessly. But every single of them could not only identify Jewish foods like gefilte fish and kugel, but could proudly offer recipes for them as well. Moral of the story: when everything else Jewish has been stripped away, it is those Jewish *tastes* that still remain on the tongue. Those first gastronomic associations with tradition, lovingly spooned by our mothers into our mouths as children, leave the deepest impressions. So as long as Moroccans Jews remember and crave the sweet taste of mofleta dripping with honey after Pesach, the *minhag* of *mimouna* will continue.

And why not? *Minhag,* or custom, is the spice of religion. It's like a twist of cardamom in an otherwise prosaic cup of coffee; it gives the whole cup a unique and exotic flavor, a taste to be remembered and savored long after the teacups are rinsed and put away.

Mofleta Recipe

2 pounds flour (about 7-8 cups)
1 teaspoon salt
2 packages or 4 ½ teaspoons dry yeast, dissolved with a
teaspoon of sugar in ½ cup very warm water
Oil

Combine the flour and salt in a large bowl; add the yeast mixture and about another 1 ½ cups water, mixing and then kneading into a smooth, soft dough. Pull off balls of dough about the size of an egg and let rise on an oiled surface for at least half an hour.

Now take a ball, oil a work surface and flatten it with oiled hands, stretching it in all directions to make a very thin, large pancake (Moroccans have no compunction about cooking with off-putting quantities of oil).

Heat a skillet over medium-high heat and brush with oil. Fry the pancakes until golden brown on each side (they tend to mottle and look like matzoh), a couple of minutes per side. I usually keep two or three skillets going at the same time during mimouna, because there are so many eager people waiting at the table for seconds and thirds. You can wrap the already-cooked mofleta in foil and keep them warm in the oven. Serve with butter, honey, jam, and/or confectioner's sugar.

Chapter 17

Lactose Tolerant: Menus for Shavuot

THERE ARE many mothers who share my daily weeknight predicament: if you serve meat, the girls say, "What? Meat *again?* Why don't you ever make *dairy?*" So the next night you decide to make it Ladies' Night and try something *halavi* (dairy), and then the boys complain: "Where's the beef? You call this a *supper?*"

I have always had a soft spot in my heart for Shavuot, the holiday that celebrates the receiving of the Torah on Mount Sinai, and one of the reasons is that the meat-versus-dairy battle is laid to rest. Our main meals are usually meat—those men need fortification for the custom of staying up all night to study Torah—but when they come home in the morning, they're all craving a big hunk of New York-style cheesecake and maybe some blintzes and dairy kugel as well!

Anyone familiar with Moroccans knows that dairy is not their strong suit, to say the least. Most of them hardly have any dairy dishes to speak of, perhaps one saucepan to make *mofleta* and another pot to make *berkoks* (the milk-and-cinnamon infused couscous traditional for Purim). Their consumption of anything dairy in Casablanca or Marrakech was limited to a café au lait in the morning and a little butter smeared on the bread—sometimes not even that, as they often dipped their morning bread in olive oil.

I used to think that my mother-in-law, she should live and be well, was an extreme case of the Moroccan aversion to dairy. She finds anything dairy, with the possible exception of chocolate ice cream, utterly revolting. I began to imagine it might be genetically based, since one of my daughters—the one who happens to share her name, Aziza—also refuses everything dairy except ice cream and pizza.

But then one night I found myself sitting with my friend Chani at a simcha. Chani is half-Moroccan but raised in America. She told me that her Morocco-born-and-raised husband is also disgusted by anything dairy. "When my kids were small, I used to drink a big glass of milk every morning, and he would look at me as if he were going to retch," she said. "I'd tell him, 'Why not? It's *good!*'

"But then," she continued, "I went with him to Morocco, and somebody let out that I wouldn't mind having some milk. Well, I have to tell you the milk they brought me had a stench like I've never smelled before! It was *awful!* Suddenly I understood why my husband thought I was crazy to like the stuff."

I have read that milk straight from a cow is actually quite good, but perhaps this unpasteurized, unhomogenized version was just too foreign for my friend's homogenized American tastes. And then again, in a torrid country where refrigeration may not always be ideal, perhaps it had simply turned rancid. Or maybe somebody brought her camel's milk by mistake!

What this doesn't explain is why Sephardim from other places—Syria, Lebanon, Greece, Italy—are far from dairy-negative. They use cheese frequently and in some very tasty dishes. Furthermore, their milk and cheese are as likely to come from a goat or sheep as from a cow, as in feta cheese. Jews from the Levant have also traditionally been big producers and consumers of yogurts and lebens. So with apologies to my Moroccan family—not to mention all those men and boys who feel that a meal without meat is no meal at all-- I had no choice but to look beyond North Africa for some dairy recipes for Shavuot.

The first Sephardic dairy item that comes to mind was samboosak, a Syrian boureka-type pastry filled with cheese. You often find them at a meal following an early-morning bris, or simply rounding out a dairy meal. A samboosak shares one important feature with a potato chip: in both cases, it's impossible to eat just one!

Then I called my Sephardic-Italian friend Leah, who told me that Italians tend to eat cheese either at the beginning of a meal, as part of an antipasto, or at the end as a sort of dessert course. "Sometimes we grate it onto pasta as well," she said, "and there are a few dishes, like lasagna, where it plays a major role." Leah then shared her recipe for *mozzarella a la caprese*, an appetizer, and her recipe for lasagna.

They ended up being good enough to win the approval of my dairy-averse Moroccan family, even those meat-loving teenage boys!

Samboosak

There are recipes for samboosak dough, but when the weather is so hot, who wants to potchke? I advise picking up the ready-to-use frozen dough in the supermarket.

2 packages samboosak dough rounds (such as Mazor's brand), defrosted
4 large eggs

2 pounds grated Muenster cheese or 3 parts grated Muenster to
1 part crumbled feta
Dash salt
2 cups sesame seeds

Combine the eggs, cheese and salt in a bowl to make a slightly dry filling mixture.

Pour the sesame seeds into a plate (half a cup at a time). Put a defrosted dough round into the plate and press to make the seeds stick in (this will flatten the disk slightly also. You can do this with a rolling pin or your hands). With the sesame-seed side down, place a tablespoon of the filling mixture in the center of the round and fold one end over to make a crescent shape; crimp the edges together with the tines of a fork. Continue making crescents in this manner and place on lightly greased baking sheets.

Bake 20-25 minutes at 350 degrees. Makes about 60.

Mozzarella a la caprese
This is a kind of open-faced layered sandwich in the style of bruschetta. "A la caprese" means shepherd-style, because this was a handy meal for shepherds to tote along while grazing their flocks.

1 baguette
3 beefsteak tomatoes
1 log of mozzarella cheese (can substitute grated or packaged mozzarella, but the logs are more authentic)
3 tablespoons extra-virgin olive oil
½ cup chopped fresh basil

Cut the baguette into slices about ½ inch thick. Slice the mozzarella into rounds, as well as the tomatoes; layer the tomatoes and then the cheese on top of the bread slices. Drizzle with the olive oil and sprinkle with the chopped basil. Bake fifteen minutes or so at 300 degrees, just enough to soften the tomatoes slightly and melt the cheese a bit. Serves 4-6.

Lasagna

1 1-pound box lasagna noodles, cooked according to package direction (or one package oven-ready lasagna noodles)
1 jar roasted garlic pasta sauce
1/2 cup chopped fresh basil
1 pound ricotta or farmer cheese
1 10-ounce box frozen chopped spinach
2 eggs
Salt, pepper
6 ounces grated mozzarella cheese

Mix together the cheese, spinach (defrosted, excess water squeezed out), eggs, salt and pepper in a bowl to make the filling.

Spoon a small amount of the pasta sauce onto the bottom of a 9 x 13 baking dish, just enough to cover. Add a layer of lasagna noodles. Dot with spoonfuls of the cheese mixture, then cover with a layer of pasta sauce sprinkled with fresh basil. Repeat the layering process: noodles, cheese, sauce and basil. When you get to the last layer of noodles, cover only with pasta sauce and the mozzarella cheese and a few basil leaves for garnish.

Bake about half an hour at 350 degrees. Feeds 6-8 people as a main course.

Chapter 18

Tisha B'Av: Lentils and Other Incidentals

OF THE ENTIRE Jewish calendar year, the Three Weeks before Tisha B'Av—the Hebrew date which commemorates the burning of the Second Temple in 70 A.D. and the resulting exile of the Jewish people—are surely the most depressing time of the year. They are depressing by design. If we didn't impose all these restrictions of mourning on ourselves we would never willingly choose to dwell on the all-too-painful recollections of this tragedy: the starvation during the siege of Jerusalem, the burning of the Temple, the captivity and exile that followed, the tremendous decline in spiritual connectedness.

Personally, I would love for the Messiah to come and end the Exile if only to get rid of the Three Weeks. You finally get to summer, and you want to relax and enjoy, and no sooner have the kids settled into a camp schedule than you have to worry about no music or swimming or anything that sounds too much like fun. And since the summer itself isn't much longer than eight weeks (in the U.S., anyway), a three-week mourning period puts a big damper on a rather sizable chunk of it. The last Nine Days of it are especially tough, because there are prohibitions on eating meat and doing laundry.

For Sephardim, the Nine Days that precede Tisha B'Av are a little easier to bear because they are usually not a full Nine Days. That is, the no-meat, no-laundry restrictions do not begin until after the Shabbat that falls during this period. "Obviously," sniffed one Sephardic friend, "we Sephardim have a shorter period where we can't do laundry because we're so much *cleaner.*"

I found this rather unfair. "I don't know about that," I replied. "I mean, maybe Sephardim *had* to wash more because they come from such hot places! It's one thing to skip laundry when you live in a cool Polish forest, another when you live in Baghdad and the temperature is 130 degrees in the shade!"

Whatever the reason, *all* Jews fnd themselves with at least a few days of dirty laundry and vegetarian meals, and we all sit down to an *erev* Tisha B'Av repast of lentils and eggs. Which is, of course, yet another downer—here we are facing a 25-hour fast, and instead of fortifying ourselves with an enormous, delectable feast as we do *erev* Yom Kippur, all there is to keep body and soul together are lentils and eggs!

On the other hand, I have to admit, I rather *like* lentils from time to time. They have a mild taste and are, mercifully, somewhat easier on the digestion than larger beans. They're also very good for you. Next to soybeans, lentils contain the highest percentage of protein of all the legumes (26 percent), and quite a lot of iron (about 3 ½ ounces of raw lentils contain 60 percent of the RDA for iron). Lentils are also virtually fat-free and are high in folate, magnesium, and fiber.

I don't make lentils often precisely because they are so strongly associated with mourning (especially the green ones), and my superstitious Moroccan extended family would be horrified to see them at a holiday meal. But the little orangey-red ones are somehow more cheerful-looking and make nice salads and soups (in soups, curiously, they melt into a greenish color). Every year I make a red lentil soup for the Shabbat of Parshat Toldot, the chapter in which Esav trades away his birthright for a bowl of red lentils, to give the kids an experiential lesson on the *parsha*. I know the soup was a success when they tell me, "Okay, Mommy, this one is worth a birthright!"

While lentils don't seem to figure much in Ashkenazic cooking, except for the occasional appearance in a mixed vegetable or bean soup, they are much more of a staple in Sephardic kitchens. The Syrians make soup with them and a rice and lentil mixture called *mejedrah*; similar to mejedrah, but with the addition of tomato sauce and cumin, is an Iraqi dish called *kitchree* that is traditional for the Nine Days. (Upon further research I found that kitchree is an Oriental dish found literally *m'Hodu v'ad Cush*—from India to Egypt, the terms the Purim Megillah uses to describe Achashverous's kingdom. It has many variations, but always involves lentils and rice.)

The only caveat with yummy lentil dishes is that, as my husband once remarked, when you make lentils *too* delicious they no longer seem appropriate for erev Tisha B'Av!

Lentil Soup
for Tisha B'Av, Parshat Toldoth, or anytime

4 cloves garlic
2 teaspoons kosher salt
2 tablespoons olive oil or cooking oil
1 small onion
1 rib celery
1 carrot
2 small potatoes
2 cups red lentils, rinsed and checked

10 cups water or pareve broth
1 teaspoon cumin
¼ teaspoon pepper
1/3 cup chopped cilantro or parsley (optional)

Put the garlic cloves through a press and mash with the salt. Heat the oil in your soup pot over medium-high heat and sauté the garlic until golden. Remove with a slotted spoon and set aside.

Chop the onion, carrot, celery and potatoes into small pieces (I use a food processor). Saute them in the remaining oil until softened. Add the lentils, broth, cumin and pepper and bring to a boil. Let boil, covered, about an hour, until lentils are mostly dissolved, stirring from time to time to make sure the lentils do not settle on the bottom and burn (This recipe is a good choice for cooking in a pressure cooker, which will reduce the cooking time to twenty minutes. If the soup seems to get too thick, add more water or broth).

Add the reserved garlic and cilantro and simmer ten minutes more. If you like a smooth texture, you can puree the soup with an immersion blender, but if you let it cook long enough the lentils will melt into mush anyway!

Kitchree

This is a very healthy version, great for vegetarians.

2 tablespoons oil or margarine
1 large onion
1 cup brown rice
1 cup dried green lentils
3 cups pareve chicken broth or water
1 8-ounce can tomato sauce

1 bay leaf
1/4 tsp. pepper
1 teaspoon cumin
½ teaspoon tumeric
1 teaspoon. salt

Heat oil or margarine in a 3-quart pot and saute onions until golden brown.

Rinse rice and lentils in a colander and drain. Add to onions and sauté for 2-3 minutes to dry them out. Add boiling water or stock, tomato sauce and seasonings. Cover and simmer over low heat until quite tender, about an hour (check after 45 minutes; if mixture is dry but not soft, add more water). Add more salt if desired; serve piping hot. Some make this in dairy pots and top with plain yogurt or fried eggs.

Part Three

Spices Of Life

Chapter 19

Food "Coloring," Part I: Turmeric

LIKE MOST MEMBERS of the fairer sex, when it comes to clothing or interior decoration, I've always been attuned to color and have well-established preferences. But I never thought very deeply into the color schemes of my food Then I entered the Sephardic world.

I still remember the first time my sister-in-law complimented a chicken dish I had made by saying, "It has such a nice color." "Color?" I thought. "Who cares about the color, as long as it tastes good?" But color *is* important. A psychologist once devised an experiment where he prepared top-quality steaks for his subjects to taste. Some of the steaks were left *au natural,* while others were dyed green or blue. You can imagine how eagerly his subjects jumped to tuck away the green and blue steaks.

On a similar note, my family once hosted a group of young Israeli women for a Friday evening meal. One of the Sephardi girls took one look at the table covered with salads of various hues and gave a loud sigh of pleasure. "Finally—food with *color!*" she exclaimed.

Barbara Bensoussan

"With color?" I repeated, not quite understanding.

"Oh, yes," she said, nodding vigorously. "Usually we go to Ashkenazim for Shabbat meals and all we eat is. . .WHITE FOOD! *Hakol lavan!* [It's all white!] White gefilte fish, white matzoh balls, white kugel and chicken, white sponge cake! We're all dying for food that has *color!*"

Now it's not really fair beat up on Ashkenazim. I explained to my guest that Eastern European cuisine comes out of cold climates where a large selection of colorful vegetables simply wasn't available, and the cooking developed accordingly. To illustrate the point, I related an account I once read about life in the village of Mir (home of the famous Mirrer Yeshiva). The woman who was interviewed said they had almost no vegetables—only potatoes, onions, beets, maybe a carrot or cucumber from time to time. Nevertheless she claimed that life in Mir was idyllic, because the people were so deeply saturated with fine Torah qualities and learning. (Fancy food isn't everything, after all). The Sephardim, on the other hand, come from Arab or Mediterranean climates that have more in common with California than Siberia and enjoy the same sort of bountiful and varied produce. They had the luxury of filling their tables with all manner of colorful vegetable and fruit dishes.

Not only that, they had a greater variety of spices to color, flavor and preserve the food. One of these, turmeric (*curcum* in Hebrew) is just about absent from Ashkenazi cooking (unless you count its presence in mustard, where it gives it the yellow color). But it pervades most of Sephardic cuisine. In fact, when I asked my Iranian friend Dalia for a Persian recipe using turmeric, she answered: "What do you mean? I put turmeric in *everything!*" It was so important to their cooking that Dalia remembers that, as a child in Shiraz, it was her job to grind turmeric roots by hand every Nissan so they could have it available *kosher l'Pesach.*

Turmeric, like saffron, dyes everything a bright yellow color, but is much cheaper than saffron. The fastidious cook should be forewarned that it will stain your clothing if you are careless with it. But it gives a lovely golden color to chicken, fish, meats, and soups. The taste is not particularly strong, but don't overdo it or you will end up with food that smells and tastes like French's mustard.

There have been some recent studies linking turmeric consumption with lower rates of Alzheimer's disease. In India, where turmeric plays a major role in the cuisine (all those curries and such), fewer than one percent of their senior citizens develop this disease. Research has shown that curcumin, the active ingredient in turmeric, not only prevents but helps reduce amyloid plaques in the brain, which are believed to cause Alzheimer's. Turmeric also contains anti-infectious and antioxidant properties. I know an older man who begins his day eating small cubes of freshly cut garlic, ginger and turmeric roots. He's convinced it keeps him vigorous and healthy, but for some strange reason can't persuade his family to join him.

So while nothing in life is guaranteed, here's yet more proof that eating Sephardic food is not only good but good for you. I will conclude with two recipes using turmeric, one for a pretty yellow-colored rice and another that is a version of a Moroccan standard, chicken with olives. They'll both add a sunshine-y burst of color to the table and a burst of flavor to your palate.

Yellow Rice
1 onion, diced
1 tablespoon oil
3 cups water or broth
1 ½ cups rice
2 teaspoons salt
¼ teaspoon turmeric

¼ cup toasted sliced or slivered almonds (optional but yummy)

Saute the onion in the oil until just beginning to brown. Add the water, salt and turmeric and bring to a boil. Add rice. Stir to mix, reduce heat to low, cover and let simmer 20-30 minutes until water is absorbed. Mix in almonds before serving.

Chicken With Olives

2 tablespoons olive oil or cooking oil
1 onion, diced
6 cloves of garlic, peeled, coarsely chopped
1 teaspoon turmeric
3-4 pounds chicken pieces (bottoms work well, but you can use the whole chicken)
Salt, pepper
1 teaspoon cumin
½ teaspoon thyme
1 teaspoon za'atar (optional)
1 tablespoon tomato paste
1 can pitted green olives
½ lemon, cut into about six pieces
¼ cup fresh parsley or cilantro

Saute onion in the oil for a few minutes over medium high heat, until transparent; add garlic. Add the turmeric and blend until the oil is uniformly yellow. Raise the heat slightly and add the chicken pieces, browning them on each side (2-3 minutes a side). As you brown the pieces, sprinkle them with salt, pepper, cumin, thyme and za'atar.

Now add two cups of water, the tomato paste, the drained olives, and the lemon pieces. Partially cover and simmer over medium-low heat for one hour, until the chicken is tender and most of the liquid has evaporated (add more water if it evaporates too fast and begins to burn). Sprinkle with parley or cilantro and serve over rice or couscous.

Chapter 20

Food Coloring Part 2: Saffron

DESPITE VASTLY DIFFERENT CULTURAL BACKGROUNDS, my Ashkenazi mother and Sephardi mother-in-law are both products of a more frugal and resourceful generation. For example, both are advocates of saving old jars from foods like applesauce and mayonnaise and re-using them to store staples like barley, white beans, split peas, and macaroni. I became rather fond of this practice myself; glass jars, unlike plastic containers, never seem to absorb odors or stains, and the lids seal tightly against dust or what one hopes is the very remote possibility of (shudder!) six-legged intruders. And on a brighter note, there is something comforting and eye-pleasing about rows of glass jars tidily lining the inside of a kitchen cabinet, filled with all manner of colorful grains and legumes.

During one of my Moroccan sister-in-law's visits I opened the refrigerator to find one of my glass jars sitting in the fridge filled with a bright orange liquid. Red spore-like filaments floated in suspension around the top and sides. "What *is* this stuff?" I cried, suspecting my sister-in-law was trying some new

130

concoction from a Chinese herbalist or dissolving a bizarrely tinted medication in water.

"Oh, it's saffron water," she said matter-of-factly. "I use it in soups sometimes, and it gives a very nice flavor to the Shabbat stew."

In response to my clueless expression, she went on to explain: "I pour boiling water over a teaspoon or so of saffron, and let it steep fifteen or twenty minutes before I use it. Whatever's left over can stay in the fridge in a jar." Now, I had once bought saffron for a recipe, and tried throwing a few threads into my chicken, but the result was unimpressive. But maybe the saffron simply hadn't had time to dissolve. It was easy to see how this vividly-colored liquid could pack a punch in terms of adding an even, orangey-yellow hue to food.

Saffron also adds a subtle flavor, a sort of grassy undertone that is suggestive rather than blatant. You wouldn't want to use too much of it at one time anyway, because saffron is, and has always been, the world's most expensive spice. Think gold is expensive? A pound of saffron threads today starts at $500 and can cost as much as $5,000! (The rest of us buy it in quantities of a gram or two at a time—my local Sephardic market sells little plastic boxes of it, tied with gold ribbon and displaying a tiny picture of Spanish ladies sitting around a table separating saffron flowers, for prices ranging between ten and fifteen dollars.) The reason for such hefty prices is that saffron consists of the dried stamens of a flower that have to be meticulously separated by hand, flower by flower. Each pound of saffron contains anywhere from 70,000 to 200,000 threads.

Saffron is one of the world's oldest spices. It is referred to by Assyrians in the 7th century B.C.E., by ancient Persians and denizens of Crete, and was cultivated by the Greeks and Chinese. My initial guess that saffron water was some sort of medical infusion was not so far off the mark either, as saffron was used in the ancient world to treat stomach problems, heal wounds and coughs, and lift bouts of depression. The vivid yellow color it produces has long been used as a fabric dye in the Orient, and more recently adorned the saffron "Gates" environmental art in Central Park.

Talk, talk, talk, when do we eat? Jews with Mediterranean roots use saffron to color and flavor rice, meats and soups. Here's a rice pilaf recipe and a soup recipe that use saffron to best advantage. The color alone will be sure to brighten your day!

Saffron Water: Dissolve one teaspoon saffron threads in one quart boiling water.

Saffron Rice:

2 tablespoons olive oil or cooking oil
1 small onion, minced
1 clove garlic, minced
1½ cups long-grain white rice
Salt, pepper
1 cup boiling water and 1 cup hot saffron water
¼ cup toasted pine nuts or almonds

Heat the oil in a saucepan with a tight-fitting lid over medium heat. Saute the onion for several minutes, until transparent; add the garlic and sauté another minute or two. Add the rice, salt and pepper and sauté the rice for a couple of minutes. Now add the hot water and saffron water to the pot, turn the heat to low, cover and let simmer about twenty minutes, or until water is absorbed and rice has softened. Mix in pine nuts and almonds (craisins are also a yummy addition).

Moroccan Chickpea Soup with Saffron

2 tablespoons light olive or other cooking oil
1 onion
1 leek (well-cleaned, white part only)
5 cloves garlic
1 rib of celery
2 carrots
1 bay leaf
1 package marrow bones (about a pound)
3-4 potatoes
2 cans chickpeas
Salt, pepper
½ teaspoon turmeric
½ teaspoon thyme
2 cups saffron water
2 cups chicken broth (or pareve chicken broth)
1/3 cup chopped parsley or cilantro

Start this soup by putting the first five vegetables into your food processor. Chop them coarsely with the steel knife and add to a soup pot whose bottom you have covered with the oil and a bay leaf. Saute these vegetables until they are softened, about five minutes, and add in the bones. Brown the bones with the vegetables. Now put the potatoes, peeled and chopped in your processor, into the pot. Add saffron water, broth and enough additional water so that all the pieces are covered and floating loosely in the liquid, and bring to a boil. While the soup is heating up, add the spices: salt and pepper, half a teaspoon of turmeric, another half teaspoon of thyme. Add the chickpeas. If you want the soup to have an especially smooth texture, slip off the outer skins from the chickpeas before adding them to the soup (just rub them gently between your fingers, and a layer of transparent skin will come off). This is a tedious process (I recommend delegating it to children), but it gives the soup a velvety consistency and makes it easier on the digestion.

Let your soup simmer for about an hour and a half, stirring occasionally because the pieces of potato and chickpeas tend to sink to the bottom and might burn if you don't check the soup from time to time. When the soup has cooked long enough to soften the meat on the bones (an hour or so), take it off the stove and let it cool slightly. Take out the bones, reserving them in a bowl. Now take out your immersion blender and whir your soup into a puree. (You can leave it half-pureed if you like a chunkier soup.) Add in the chopped cilantro and the reserved marrow bones. A great, rib-sticking recipe for a wintery Friday night!

Chapter 21

Food Coloring Part III: Paprika

ONE OF THE gifts I received when I became engaged was Viviane and Nina Moryoussef's book *Moroccan Jewish Cookery*, a big, beautiful book sporting glossy photos of Moroccan specialties temptingly displayed in traditional tagine pots and painted ceramic plates. But a few things in the book confounded me. For one, the measurements were always European-style, in kilos and grams instead of pounds and tablespoons, difficult for mathematically challenged folks like me to convert. Even more quaintly, sometimes the measurements were given, rather than in cups, in quantities of "mustard glasses," e.g., "add two mustard glasses of water and one of oil and mix. . ." I have since learned that in Morocco everyone used to buy the same brand of Dijon mustard in glass jars, and so those jars eventually took on the status of a standard measure.

Another point of confusion was that the recipes often called for either "sweet paprika," "hot paprika," or both. At the time, as far as I knew, there was only one paprika: the red stuff that comes in big plastic spice containers in the supermarket, and which adds color but not very much flavor to food. "Hot paprika" didn't seem to be the same thing as chili powder, and in the quantities it was called for, I didn't think it was cayenne pepper either. But eventually, having gotten myself off to an Israeli grocery, I discovered that there are even more than those two paprika options. Israeli companies such as Pereg manufacture powdered sweet and hot paprika, and in case that isn't sufficient, they offer paprika mixed with oil and two grades of paprika flakes, coarse and fine, also mixed with a bit of oil. I have tried the flakes and find that they dissolve after long cooking, leaving only a nice rich color. The powdered hot paprika seems a shade milder than cayenne pepper but will still pack a punch to spicy foods.

Paprika comes from dried, ground peppers, and the name "paprika" comes from linguistic derivatives of the word "pepper." The peppers used today in paprika are native to the New World and were brought to Europe by explorers. They were easily adopted by the Old World, as they thrive in many climates, but they grow especially well in warmer ones. In the U.S., most paprika comes from the Southwest, while in Europe, Hungary became known for the superior quality of its paprika (which is surely how chicken *paprikash* came to a signature dish of Hungarian cuisine).

Paprika gets heavy use in Sephardic cooking because, as I have mentioned, Sephardim like their food to have a nice color, and nothing beats paprika for giving a roasted-red color to meats and sauces. And since Sephardim also like a little more zing in their dishes, hot paprika steps in to turn up the heat. Ready for a few examples of Sephardic recipes using paprika? Well, if I haven't confused you too much already with all these different grades of paprika, then let me confuse you again by offering two similar-sounding, paprika-using recipes for your consideration: *harissa* and *shakshouka*.

Shakshouka, which I am told is of Tunisian origin, is a dish of eggs cooked with stewed tomatoes, peppers and onions, and its current name derives from the Hebrew *l'shakshek*, or "to shake." It has become popular in Israel as the quintessential any-time meal, performing equally well for breakfast, lunch, snack time, or a light supper.

As for harissa, every time my mother –in-law comes to visit, she leaves me with a recipe that my family has become so enamored of that I find myself obliged to keep reproducing it no matter how much extra time it consumes. Her "harissa" is one such dish.

Harissa is a Moroccan cooked salad of red peppers and garlic. It is similar to the Yemenite s'chug, which is basically pureed hot peppers, garlic and oil and is guaranteed to put, if not a tiger in your tank, a dragon in your mouth. My mother-in-law's version isn't exactly like the harissa found in restaurants or stores, which is ground more finely and is usually fiery hot. This version can be made mild or hot but is delicious either way.

Shakshouka

2 tablespoons olive or other cooking oil
1 large onion
1 clove garlic, chopped
1 bell pepper, diced (I like to use ½ green and ½ red)
1 28-ounce can crushed tomatoes
1 tablespoon tomato paste
1 teaspoon sweet (regular) paprika
¼ teaspoon hot paprika (optional), or a few slices of chopped jalapeno pepper
6 eggs
Salt, pepper
¼ cup parsley or cilantro for garnish (optional)

Over medium heat, sauté onion, pepper and garlic until beginning to brown. Add the crushed tomatoes and tomato paste along with the two kinds of paprika and cook, covered, for twenty minutes, adding a little water if necessary. Uncover and pour the eggs on top of the tomatoes. Cover and cook another five minutes, then cook uncovered until the egg whites have turned white. Garnish with an additional shake of paprika, parsley or cilantro, and serve hot.

Harissa

8-10 red peppers, seeded and cut into chunks
2 tablespoons oil
2 cloves garlic
1 teaspoon sweet paprika
1 teaspoon hot paprika (or to taste)
1 teaspoon cumin
2 teaspoons white vinegar
Salt, to taste (about a teaspoon)

Puree your red peppers in a food processor (this is the time-consuming part). You'll have to keep scraping down the sides, and it won't be a perfectly smooth puree—that's okay—and it will take two or three batches to grind all the peppers. If you're a fan of hot salsas, then you might want to grind up a jalapeno pepper or ancho chile along with your bell peppers, but I leave this to your own discretion (and risk).

Dump the ground peppers with the excess water into a saucepan and let them simmer for an hour or so until the water is almost completely evaporated. Now add a couple of table-spoons of oil, two cloves of garlic run through a press, a teaspoon of hot paprika (or to taste), a teaspoon of cumin, a little salt and let it simmer another fifteen minutes or so. When you're done cooking the mixture, mix in a teaspoon of white vinegar. That's it!

Like tchouktchouka, this stuff is heavenly spread on fresh challah, and it also is wonderful in sandwiches, omelettes, and as a topping for focaccia or pizza. I've even mixed it with olive oil and used it to dress noodles. My mother-in-law mixes it with fried eggplant slices, and it's a nice condiment for fish.

Chapter 22

A Spice for all Seasonings: Allspice

ASHKENAZIM WHO ARE unacquainted with the Sephardic world have a tendency to lump Sephardim all together in one big undifferentiated blob labeled "those other, often darker-skinned, unfamiliar Jews." But Sephardim see their differences quite clearly, and would never confuse a Persian with a Syrian or a North African or a Yemenite. In the same way a Galitzianer might be offended if you confused him with a Yekkeh (German) or a Hungarian or a Litvak, each Sephardic group has its own particular history, personality, and, of course, cuisine.

Not to mention loyalty to its own manner of food preparation. "I don't much like Syrian food," a Moroccan friend of mine once sniffed. "They hardly make any salads like we do. And they put that spice—what's it called? Oh yeah, allspice—into *everything*." Everything? The claim seemed a little exaggerated. But when I did a little research, I found my friend was actually not so far off the mark! Barely a Syrian recipe exists that doesn't contain at least a dash of allspice.

So what exactly *is* allspice? Well, FYI, allspice is a

brownish powder that is ground from the dried, unripe berries of a bush in the myrtle family. It is grown primarily in Central America and the Caribbean, and legend has it that Columbus himself brought it back to the Old World after his travels. Since Columbus and his friends thought the berries resembled peppercorns, they named the spice "pimento," from the word "pimienta" or pepper.

The English chose to rename it "allspice" because the ground berries were considered to smell like a combination of cloves, nutmeg, cinnamon, and pepper. The English used it to flavor cakes and puddings; the Germans, while not adopting it widely in their home cooking, began using it heavily in sausage making. In the New World, allspice became part of the spice blend of Mexican mole sauces, while the people of the Caribbean incorporated it into their trademark jerk seasoning.

But, as the eternal question goes, what about the Jews? Allspice was picked up by both Jews, Arabs, and Christians of the Northern Mediterranean coast (Greece, Turkey, Syria), largely as a flavoring for meats and stews. It wasn't long before it became a ubiquitous element of Syrian Jewish cuisine.

For diplomatic reasons, I am no longer allowed to tolerate snarky remarks about Syrian foods—that is, not since four of our children married into Syrian families. Our newly official, deepened connection with the Syrian community has increased my awareness of the varieties and pleasures of gourmet Syrian cuisine, as did some of the gorgeous cookbooks my daughters received as gifts. Furthermore, my daughters, as new brides eager to learn to cook the things their husbands like to eat, have busily absorbed as many recipes as they can for Syrian specialties. Most of them—surprise, surprise—call for allspice.

One easy and healthy dish they picked up is called *libkusa*, or squash. It's a simple side dish of sautéed onions and zucchini, both healthful and reasonably dietetic. If you want to dress it up and don't mind a few extra calories, throw beaten eggs and cheese on top of it and bake it in the oven to make a sort of crustless quiche.

A somewhat more complicated, but ever so Syrian, dish is *lachemagine*, the little pizza-type meat pies served at absolutely every Syrian Kiddush. The special flavor of lachemagine comes from allspice and tamarind sauce, which is a condiment you can find in Sephardic grocery stores (it comes from the fruit of the tamarind tree, which is related to the date palm and native to Asia and Africa). If you like the sweet-sour flavor of stuffed cabbage, you'll like the flavor of lachemagine. It's sweet and meaty and it's all too easy to keep popping one after another of those cute little pizzas into your mouth as you sit shmoozing at a *simcha* table. . .

And if you decide that, like my Moroccan friend, you don't actually like allspice in your meat mixtures, don't throw it out the bottle; pumpkin season will come around and allspice works just great in pumpkin pies, sweet potato and orange squash dishes, and spice cakes!

Libkusa

2 large zucchini squash
2 onions
2 tablespoons olive oil or cooking oil
¼ teaspoon allspice (or more to taste)
Salt, pepper

Dice the onions and sauté them over medium-high heat until transparent. Add the zucchini, peeled and diced into one-inch chunks, and continue sautéing, stirring occasionally, until zucchini.is soft, about fifteen minutes. Add spices and cook another few minutes.

Variation: Libkusa "quiche"

Place the prepared zucchini into an ovenproof dish. Beat 4-5 eggs and pour over the zucchini. Top with shredded cheese of your choice. Bake in a 375 degree oven for 45 minutes, or until eggs are puffy and set and casserole has browned.

Lachemagine

[The filling in this recipe is modified from Rae Dayan's *For the Love of Cooking*. Mrs. Dayan gives a recipe for the dough as well, but today most busy cooks are just as happy to buy frozen mini-pizza dough rounds (Mazor's is a popular kosher brand). Alternatively, you can make (or buy) any recipe for pizza dough, roll it out and cut it into 3-inch circles with a drinking glass.]

Dough:
2 packages frozen mini-pizza dough rounds, mostly defrosted

Filling:
1 pound ground beef
¾ cup tamarind sauce (available in Oriental groceries)
1 tablespoon oil
½ teaspoon allspice
½ teaspoon cinnamon
1 teaspoon salt
½ teaspoon pepper
1 large onion, finely chopped
Pine nuts (pignolias--optional)

Preheat oven to 400 degrees and grease several large baking

trays. Mix all filling ingredients together except the pine nuts. Spread about a tablespoon of filling on each dough round and garnish with a few pine nuts. Bake for 15-20 minutes, until dough begins to brown.

Tip: One woman I know sandwiches two lachemagine patties together before she bakes them. She claims they come apart evenly after cooking and it helps keep the filling from drying out in the oven.

Chapter 23

Only Real Men Eat Za'atar

SINCE NEITHER MY husband nor myself grew up in New York, both of us were initially quite baffled by the Brooklyn custom of packing out to country bungalow colonies in the summers. To me, the idea of packing up my entire household sounded daunting—half exodus from Egypt and half making Pesach all over again—with the dubious "reward" being the privilege of living for two months in a cramped, dilapidated shack with capricious plumbing. (We were equally shocked to learn how much said shacks cost to rent!) As for my husband, the prospect of spending a summer separated from his wife and children sounded more like a punishment than a relief, and those three-hour commutes back and forth from the city didn't exactly sweeten the pot either.

So we always just stayed home and tried to think up various day trips to get out of the city on Sundays. Those day trips meant packing up a copious meal or two, and it became our family *minhag* to pick up fresh pita bread on our way out of the city from a Syrian bakery on Kings Highway. One morning my husband returned to the car with not only fresh pita, but a couple of other bags of pita covered with some kind of oily, greenish paste. "They have za'atar bread today!" he announced triumphantly.

The boys eyed it suspiciously. "It's *green*," they said.

"It looks *greasy*," said the girls, wrinkling their noses with disdain. But several hours later, once they were all good and hungry and we had spread out our picnic lunch, it was easier to persuade them to try it. The result? Oh brave new world! It was love at first bite! The pita, which was very fresh, had been slathered with a mixture of za'atar and olive oil, and the warm, savory taste was addictive.

Before long we were all fighting over the last morsels. But the next time we went to buy it, the bakery was almost sold out of it and there wasn't really enough to go around. So my husband and sons confiscated it for themselves, declaring, "Only *men* eat za'atar!" This of course raised a storm of feminine protest, and to this day this refrain has remained as a standing family joke. Real men may not eat quiche, but they certainly love their za'atar!

Very funny, you say, but what is this za'atar stuff? If you're not Israeli or Sephardi, you probably have no idea what it is. But if it makes you feel any better, let me confess that I have both tasted it and read up on it, and I *still* don't know what it is; the more I researched, the more elusive it became. Za'atar is really a mix of spices, in the manner of Moroccan *ras al hanout* or Indian *garam masala*; its composition varies somewhat depending on who has prepared it and where.

Most sources identify za'atar as a spice blend based around some variety of marjoram or "Syrian oregano." Other sources identify it as hyssop. It is then mixed with thyme and/or sage and/or sumac, sesame seeds and salt. Pereg, Pyramid and other Israeli manufacturers now market it, which will surely help standardize its composition and flavor for the general public.

The Lebanese believe that za'atar sharpens the mind and strengthens the body (which surely explains why the males in my family were so eager to grab it away so ungraciously). They even encourage their children to eat za'atar bread before exams. Maimonides, on the other hand, recommends za'atar as a cold remedy and an intestinal regulator. My Moroccan mother-in-law, who is hardly an expert on the Rambam, nevertheless steeps za'atar in boiling water and uses the resulting tisane to chase stomach upsets. (As much as I like za'atar, this is one form of preparation that I can guarantee you is less than appealing. On the other hand, I imagine that a hot fresh za'atar pita could go a long way towards restoring someone who's under the weather!)

Za'atar is wonderful on bread, but it is also great with hummus, with plain yogurt or feta cheese, or rubbed on meat. Today you can buy hummus pre-sprinkled with za'atar. I often add it to cooked olives and chicken with olives, and it's also good on chicken destined for the grill. Here are a few recipes for enjoying za'atar. Hey, it's never too late to go green!

Za'atar Pita

Bread:

1/2 teaspoon dry yeast dissolved in ¼ cup warm water

1 ¾ cups flour plus extra for kneading

1 teaspoon salt

2 tablespoons olive oil

¼ cup water

Za'atar mixture:

3 tablespoons za'atar mixed with 1/3 cup extra-virgin olive oil

Combine flour and salt in a bowl; add olive oil and work it into the flour with your fingers. Add the yeast-in-water mixture, then the remaining ¼ cup water, and knead briefly into a sticky dough. Let rest 15 minutes, covered, then knead dough for several minutes until smooth, adding a little flour if necessary. Shape into a ball and let rise one hour.

Divide dough into four balls and preheat a nonstick skillet over medium heat. Preheat the broiler as well. Now flatten each ball into a pita round with a rolling pin, dimpling the dough with your fingers to keep the toppings from running off. Transfer a pita to the skillet spread with a quarter of the za'atar and oil mixture. Cook about three minutes, until the bottom is crisp and golden; now brown the top surface under the broiler. Repeat with remaining rounds.

For those who feel life is too short to make your own pita, you can simply make the za'atar/olive oil mix and spread it on store-bought pita. Then pop it under the broiler for a minute or two.

Za'atar Pita Chips and Hummus

Ingredients
4-5 large pita rounds, cut into small triangles
1-2 cloves fresh garlic, run through a press
1/3 cup olive oil
3 teaspoons za'atar
Home-made or store-bought hummus, for dipping
Preheat oven to 350-400 degrees.

In a small saucepan, heat the olive oil with the garlic for several minutes, then add the za'atar. Place pita triangles onto a baking sheet and brush the oil mixture onto tops of them. Place in oven for about 10-15 minutes (depending upon how crisp you like the pita). Serve with a bowl of hummus as a dip.

Za'atar Chicken Thighs
8 chicken thighs, skin on

Olive oil (about 1/3 cup)
Za'atar
Kosher salt
Garlic powder

Preheat oven to 425. Brush chicken thighs with olive oil, then sprinkle liberally with za'atar. Add salt and garlic powder to taste. Bake fifteen minutes at 425, then reduce heat to 375 and bake forty-five minutes longer, until chicken is tender.

Note: You could roast an entire chicken this way. For a 3-4 pound chicken, roast at 425 for twenty minutes and then at 375 for another hour. Stuff the cavity with half a lemon to hold the shape and add flavor.

Part Four

Assorted Tidbits

Chapter 24

Cooking Under Pressure

MOST MOROCCAN DISHES—THE cooked salads, the soups, the *tagines* (stews)—are what they call in French *plats mijotes*, that is, dishes that simmer for hours on the stove. This used to present problems for me on *erev yom tov*, as I have only four burners on my stove and would find I had to start putting various dishes on a wait list for the next free burner. I contemplated getting a stove with six burners, but then reality reared its ugly head and I realized that, finances aside, my tiny Brooklyn kitchen simply didn't have the space to accommodate that gorgeous six-burner, double-oven Viking stove I'd drooled over in cooking magazines.

I was also puzzled by the fact that Moroccans, who live in a climate so hot that the breakfast butter is already soupy at eight in the morning, had a cuisine that required so many hours of stove top time. Could it be simply another sadistic Arab conspiracy to make women's lives miserable, right up there with illiteracy, honor killings and having to wear a burka? It's bad enough to be forcibly confined to the house, but how much worse when that house has become superheated because the temperature outside is already a hundred degrees in the shade and your lunch menu required three hours' simmer time on the stove!

My sister-in-law, who hates to cook and is always looking for ways to cut down time in the kitchen, gave me the solution. "In Morocco everybody uses a *cocotte minute* [pressure cooker]," she said. "How do you get by without one? You lose way too much time with regular pots!"

My mother-in-law agreed, adding in her own two cents (or shekels). "You waste so much money on gas for the stove without the *cocotte*," she said disapprovingly. "When the food cooks faster, you consume much less." Now that was a concept that never would have occurred to me on my own; the mysterious gas bills I receive lump together the heat and the stove and are anyway always astronomical. But in Morocco, they didn't need gas heat and bought gas for the stove in canisters, which meant their actual consumption could be seen in canisters per month.

My own mother had never used a pressure cooker, and being a technology-challenged person, I was intimidated by the idea of figuring out a new gadget. Somehow I was under the impression a pressure cooker was something either electric or complicated (it is neither). My husband also discouraged me from pursuing the idea, pleading PTSD from the memory of being a toddler in his mother's arms when a pressure cooker exploded in their kitchen, making a noise like a truck bomb and coating the walls and ceiling with a sludge of meat and fava beans. People reassured me the newer pressure cookers are designed with safety features to avoid precisely this type of disaster, but nevertheless I successfully avoided buying a *cocotte* for many years, until one year my mother-in-law came for Pesach and in a combination of exasperation and compassion bought me one and showed me how to use it.

My friends, she made a convert out of me! What a wonderful, magical gadget! It cooks everything in one-third the time (for such is the rule of thumb, I discovered once I researched it). It speeds up the cooking time for potatoes, beets, beans. It can literally save the day if the need suddenly arises to produce a dish posthaste. One recent example: I was making a carrot soup for Shabbat, and foolishly decided it needed just a hint of consommé powder. So I gave the container a little shake to add those few granules of powder, and a huge lump fell in! I couldn't manage to fish it out before it had dissolved and left my soup with a revolting taste of way too much MSG and artificial flavoring. I tried diluting it with water, with potato flakes, with soy milk—nothing helped. So I dumped the whole mess, *kapparah* [it should be atonement], and with the clock ticking with hour till Shabbat threw some chicken and vegetables into my pressure cooker and half an hour later had a chicken soup that my children found a delightful change from our usual Sephardic vegetable soups.

The pressure cooker is a boon for working moms. Unless you are one of those Superwomen who cooks a week's worth of food on Sundays or manages to put supper into a crock pot every morning before leaving for work (a level of forethought and organization well beyond my own limited capacities), you probably come home having to rustle up fast suppers like fried cutlets or broiled fish or meat (or, let's be honest, pizza from the pizza store). But the pressure cooker allows you a much greater variety of menus: beef stew, chicken and potatoes, bean soups, etc, which can be ready in as long as it takes to fry a platter of chicken cutlets.

The newer, slicker pressure cookers can run about a hundred dollars and change in appliance stores, but mine is a forty-dollar Chinese model from a discount store that has a nice heavy bottom and works just fine. You can find more information on how to use them—recipes, time charts, safety tips—in cookbooks and Internet sites. It's a worthwhile investment even if you have an electric stove and won't be saving on gas bills.

Because (funny as it sounds), a pressure cooker takes a lot of the pressure *off* the busy cook!

Fast Chicken with Potatoes

1 chicken cut in eighths
2 large onions, cut into chunks
5 cloves garlic
2 tablespoons cooking oil
1 teaspoon turmeric (curcum)
1 teaspoon paprika
½ teaspoon hot paprika (or to taste)
1.2 teaspoon cumin
Salt, pepper
8 large potatoes, peeled and cut into chunks

Heat the oil in the bottom of the pressure cooker and brown the onion in it over medium-high heat until onions are staring to brown. Add the garlic and turmeric, stirring to color the oil yellow. Now add the chicken and brown on both sides (3-4 minuntes per side), sprinkling each side with the remaining spices as it browns.

Add in the potatoes and a cup and a half of water. Close pressure cooker according to the manufacturer's directions, and when steam begins to come out of the valve, cap the valve, turn down the heat, and let simmer for twenty minutes. Open carefully as per directions!

Spicy Chickpeas

A great alternative for a *shalom zachar*, the informal Friday night party that celebrates the birth of a baby boy, during which chickpeas are customarily served. It sure beats the usual offering of chickpeas served straight from the can!

1 ½ cups dried chickpeas, soaked for at least six hours (overnight is best)
2 cups water
1/3 cup oil or olive oil
2 teaspoons salt
¼ teaspoon turmeric
2 teaspoons paprika
½-1 teaspoon hot paprika or cayenne pepper
6 cloves garlic, coarsely chopped
1 red pepper, diced
¼ cup fresh cilantro, chopped

Combine all ingredients except the cilantro in the pressure cooker. Bring to a boil, close the pot and cook under pressure for 25 minutes. If the mixture is watery when the cooker is opened, you can let it simmer a little longer to reduce. Sprinkle with cilantro. Best served warm.

Chapter 25

The Mediterranean Diet

WHILE FASHIONS in clothing come and go with regularity, this is no less true of food. One year has everyone running out to buy a wok, the next to bring home a couscous steamer. People my age remember when nobody had heard of Thai cooking or sun-dried tomatoes, and sushi had not yet become standard fare Jewish at weddings (as if Japanese people would ever serve kugel and brisket at *their* affairs. But then, by the same token, when did you ever hear of Chinese people running a *Jewish* auction?).

Here's another example: once upon a time in America, it was an embarrassment to be a poor Italian immigrant; people made fun of their pasta-heavy diets and singsong accents. But today, the children of the same WASP snobs who so heartlessly mocked the immigrants are lining up and fighting each other to wrangle reservations for hot new upscale restaurants that serve —guess what?---Italian peasant food! Artisanal pasta and arti-chokes! They even go to Tuscany and purchase the crumbling farm houses the real peasants were all too happy to abandon, although instead of sleeping with the goats on the floor they put in central heating and Viking ranges. Not that they start cooking themselves, Heaven forbid—more likely they hire some local to furnish the chic regional cuisine when their friends jet in to visit.

The new appreciation for Mediterranean cuisine comes not only from a certain American veneration of European culture but a substantial amount of research that suggests that the "Mediterranean diet" happens to be a very healthy way to eat. It involves all sorts of salubrious elements such as olive oil, garlic, fish, fresh vegetables, and moderate amounts of wine with meals. ("Mediterranean-schmediterranean," I can just hear my grandmother saying, "so long as you finish your vegetables.") Personally, I'm not sure the so-called Mediterranean diet on its own deserves all the credit for prolonging the lives of the people who created it. After all, think about it: those folks are basically living on the *Riviera* their whole lives! Their days are spent in places full of sunshine and beaches and relaxed people sipping expresso in cafes!

But lest this seem too shallow, let's also remember that the Mediterranean coast has been host to a Jewish population for thousands of years, both in the north (Spain, France, Italy, Greece, Turkey, Lebanon) and the south (Morocco, Algeria, Tunisia, Libya, Egypt). Most of this population is Sephardic, having left Spain after the expulsion of 1492; many families have local roots that go back even further. My friend Ilanit, who grew up near Naples, explained to me that the king of Spain used to be the king of Naples as well, and their local dialect is sort of a Spanish version of Italian. Today, she says, many of the old shuls have closed down, and aside from a few Chabad-Lubavitch centers, there isn't much in the way of religious community.

And the cooking? For those who have not yet checked out nouvelle Italian cuisine, either in trendy food magazines or pricey restaurants, it may come as something of a revelation that real authentic Italian food—at least from the northern provinces—has little to do with pizza and spaghetti-and-meatballs. In fact, most of it requires no red sauce whatsoever. (Red-and-white checked tablecloths and candles in Chianti bottles are also optional, being largely American fabrications.)

"We believe in using seasonal ingredients, and letting their flavor shine through," Ilanit says. "We don't mask them with a lot of spices, just a few herbs like basil or oregano. Pasta and beans were our staples, and fish. Chicken was for holidays, and meat, which we had maybe once a week, was served in small portions cooked with vegetables. Eating an entire steak would be unheard of!"

The recipes my friend gave me are healthy, unfussy, and—*mamma mia!*—very delicious.

Pesce al Cartoccio (Fish in parchment)
6 small fish (river fish like mackerel are best)
6 cloves garlic, sliced
3 tablespoons olive oil
Salt, pepper
¼ cup fresh chopped parsley

Place each fish in the middle of a square of parchment paper or foil. Brush with olive oil and sprinkle with salt, pepper, garlic slices and parsley. Fold the paper or foil around the fish to make a packet. Bake at 350 degrees for twenty minutes; serve each person his own individual packet of fish.

Cannelini Bean Salad
1 can cannellini beans
1 clove garlic, sliced
1 rib of celery, diced

Salt

1 tablespoon olive oil

Juice of half a lemon

Lightly smash the cannelini beans with a fork or potato masher—the beans should still retain some of their shape. Mix in the other ingredients; serve on lettuce leaves.

Zucchini dorati fritti (fried zucchini)

2 medium zucchini

3 eggs

¼ cup flour

½ teaspoon baking powder

2 teaspoons salt (or to taste)

Olive oil for frying

Wash zucchini well but do not peel. Cut it the long way into ¼" thick slices, then cut the slices into shorter lengths (about four inches long). Whisk remaining ingredients together to make a batter. Coat zucchini slices with the batter and fry until golden. Alternative: The fried slices can also be layered with tomato sauce and fresh basil and baked for 15 minutes.

Chapter 26

Sephardic Snacking

I HAVE ALREADY WRITTEN about my year of living dangerously, that is, undertaking to accept the "gift" of a live-in Arab maid sent straight to me from Morocco by my sister-in-law. Fatima cleaned my house better than a white tornado, but her mood swings bordered on the bipolar if not completely deranged, and we spent the better parts of a year living in a tense-- but immaculately clean!-- household.

Despite her borderline personality, Fatima could be quite shrewd, and despite her biases against America her observations occasionally hit the mark. One observation that has stayed with me was her comment, delivered with a mixture of incredulity and disdain, that "Americans have everything, but they don't know how to *live*." In other words, we have a lot of possessions, but we're working too hard to enjoy them; our stores are loaded with food, but instead of eating well we subsist on pizza, Coke, and bags of potato chips.

The commercial, helter-skelter nature of American eating comes as a shock to people used to a saner rhythm of life. In Morocco, as in many places in Europe and Israel still, the major meal of the day is at noon, when all business establishments close down for two hours to allow for a leisurely lunch and perhaps a snooze. When my mother-in-law visits us in Brooklyn, she wakes up in the morning and immediately begins preparing a large hot lunch for my husband, who works close enough to come home to eat. "He needs to eat, he *works*," she says seriously, which never fails to amuse me: you'd think sitting in front of a computer all morning is the new power workout.

But in the Old Country of Morocco, lunch (more accurately called *dinner*) was an *event*, distinguished by an embroidered tablecloth, china plates (who had paperware?) and proper French table manners (with the exception of my father-in-law, of blessed memory, who to the chagrin of his children sometimes opted to use his fingers instead of his fork. "But it's even more hygienic," he would counter in protest. "The forks get used by everyone. My fingers only get used by me!").

Such family meals were properly called *dining*, not simply grabbing a meal. They elevated the act of eating into a mixture of gastronomic pleasure and family lunch date. What a far cry from our fragmented, hurried "family" meals of today, where six o'clock finds the older boys still in yeshiva eating institutional food doused with ketchup, the husband still at work for an hour or just beginning the commute home, and the younger ones already full from the macaroni and tuna—the only foods they like—that they downed when they tumbled in from school at four thirty

One advantage of a well-prepared meal consumed in a pleasant, unhurried way is that everyone leaves the table *satisfied*. As a college student, I spent a summer in France, and was impressed by the way French women ate heartily at meals, yet suffered no apparent damage to their waistlines. Then I realized that by virtue of eating beautifully prepared, well-rounded meals, these women did not feel the need to stuff their mouths all day long with nacho chips and chocolate bars. This was a life-altering epiphany; after that summer I resolved to cut short any American-style obsessing about dieting and focus instead on eating good, sensible food, paying more attention to hunger and satiety than to calories. Over the years this approach to weight control has served me pretty well, although no one is exactly banging down my door asking me to model *haute couture*.

For Jews in Arab countries, American-style snacks simply weren't available, at least not in kosher form. "*Snacks?*" say my friends who grew up in Iran or Tunisia or Lebanon. "What snacks? We took some dates, maybe a handful of nuts!" When my husband went to the movie theaters as a boy, the floors were littered not with candy bar wrappers, but shells of pumpkin and sunflower seeds. Prepackaged food barely existed; people went to the marketplace toting their own string bags and bought produce wrapped in old newspapers. Lacking preservatives and packing facilities and, in some cases, even refrigeration, the food by necessity was fresh and unaltered. My guess is that the fruits and vegetables were also more appealing and better-tasting, not having being specially bred to withstand long train rides from California or Florida and having been picked when ripe instead of rock-hard.

But, the reader asks, what about that famous Arab hospitality? What happened when an unexpected guest dropped by for one of those silver pots of sweet mint tea poured into little gold-rimmed glasses patterned with arabesques? Didn't he or she require a little extra refreshment? Well, assuming he wasn't invited for an entire meal, he might be privileged to be served some homemade cookies, a bowl of fruit, nuts or roasted seeds, olives, or pickled vegetables, perhaps a *confiture* (jam) made of eggplant, carrots, or quince. Still a far cry—and much healthier

—than the candy corn, licorice, taffy, sour sticks, etc. that are such indispensable parts of "Shabbos party," or the packaged cookies most of us keep on hand for emergencies.

I will therefore be a good Sephardic balabusta (or *shaatra*, as the Syrians say) and make sure to give you some good snack foods to eat. First will be a recipe for sweet *ka'ak* biscuits. These can also be made in a salty version and are traditionally served at yahrzeit meals commemorating the death of a loved one (like bagels, they are ring-shaped), or any other time you get the yen. If you prefer a flat cookie, the dough can be rolled out and cut into rounds. (Notch the edges with a fork if you want them to look more authentically Sephardi.) The second recipe is my own version of a pickled vegetable, a cauliflower salad that everybody seems to like for the sweet-salty dressing and crunchy texture. I've been asked for the recipe more times than I can remember, so to anyone who ever asked, here it is.

Sweet Ka'ak

These are meant to be crunchy rather than soft, perfect for dipping in a glass of tea. They will keep for weeks in a cookie tin.

3 eggs
¾ cup sugar
1 cup oil
1 teaspoon vanilla
1 teaspoon orange or lemon rind
¾ teaspoon salt
1 ½ teaspoons baking powder
3 cups flour
1 tablespoons anise seeds
1 tablespoon sesame seeds
Apricot jam (optional)

Blend together the eggs and sugar, then add the oil, vanilla and rind. Once combined well, add in the salt, baking powder, flour and seeds (the seeds can be omitted if you prefer). Knead into a smooth dough. Break off pieces of dough to make two-inch balls. Roll balls into ropes and join the ends to make a circle; alternatively, you can roll out the dough and cut out rounds with a biscuit cutter or drinking glass. For a shiny surface, brush with strained apricot jam thinned with a little hot water.

Bake on lightly greased trays at 350 degrees for about 30 minutes, or until browned.

Marinated Cauliflower Salad

1 head of cauliflower, cleaned and checked, cut into florets
1 large onion, sliced thin
2 carrots, peeled and sliced thinly on the diagonal

Marinade:
1 clove of garlic, minced or pressed
1 ½ tablespoons sugar
1 ½ teaspoons salt
dash pepper
3 tablespoons water
2/3 cup white vinegar
½ cup salad oil

Mix ingredients for the marinade in a container with a well-fitting lid (I use a square Tupperware-type container). Then add the carrots, onion and cauliflower. Shake up the mixture and let it marinate for several hours (I usually make this salad on Friday morning to serve in the evening).

Chapter 27

Alone In My Kitchen with an Eggplant

"ALONE IN MY KITCHEN WITH AN EGGPLANT" was originally the title of an essay by Laurie Colwin, a writer who left this world much too early—in her late forties—having left behind two collections of wry and often hilarious essays about cooking (*Home Cooking* and *More Home Cooking*). Although I never met Laurie, I always felt a certain kinship with her; like me, she was a nice Jewish girl from Philadelphia with culinary and literary inclinations, and she relished a new food discovery as much as she relished poking gentle fun at the strange food foibles of the arty people she frequented.

Anyway, like Laurie, I often find myself sitting alone in the kitchen with an eggplant. It is not a vegetable I grew up with; back in Philly in the 1960's, we had potatoes, peas, corn, string beans. . . but *eggplant?* I don't think they grew eggplants in Bialystok and Lvov and those other Eastern European towns my family hailed from. I first discovered eggplant as a teenager in the form of eggplant parmagiana at a bat mitzvah party, and from there it was love at first bite.

Eggplants, the botanists tell us, originated in India, and weren't introduced to Europe until about 1500. Even then, they mostly remained in warmer Mediterranean climates. While most of us are familiar with eggplants in purplish-black hues, they can be green or pink or yellow or white (it is apparently from the yellow and white ones that the name "eggplant" arose—after all, the other shades have nothing the least bit eggy about them). Eggplants also come in different shapes and sizes, from long and skinny Chinese ones to little ones just a smidgen bigger than your thumb.

My mother-in-law uses the tiny ones to make eggplant "jam," which are really candied eggplants. I know it sounds bizarre—might as well make jams from broccoli while you're at it—but by the time those eggplants have simmered for hours with sugar and spices they don't taste like eggplant at all, and you'd think you were eating a very gooey, syrupy plum.

But most of us are more accustomed to savory versions of eggplant, if we eat eggplant at all. Since *hatzilim* [their Hebrew name] grow well in Israel and have been a staple of Sephardic cooking for centuries, anyone who has been to Israel or an Israeli restaurant will have tasted *babaghanoush* or some other sautéed eggplant salad. One of the beauties of eggplant is that it lends itself to so many different types of preparation: steaming, roasting, frying.

But Let the Fryer Beware! Eggplant is nature's own oil sponge! If an ant can carry ten times its own weight in food on its back, I think an eggplant can absorb ten times its own weight in oil. As far as I can tell the only way to minimize this problem is to keep the oil really, really hot when frying (and do this preferably while your toddler is fast asleep). Oil absorption will also diminish if you salt the cut eggplant and let it sit for twenty minutes before frying; the eggplant will "weep" excess moisture and bitterness, and you will have less cause to weep as you watch hundreds of calories' worth of oil being sucked up by your simmering slices. Through bitter and oily experience, I have also discovered that if you have to sauté eggplant cubes, it pays to steam them first until tender, then sauté quickly in a little oil.

Eggplant is the tofu of vegetables: peel one and you get a white and spongy hunk that, like tofu, has a relatively neutral flavor that blends well with meat or dairy and takes on the flavors of other ingredients. Like tofu, eggplant's meaty texture adds heft to vegetarian stews like ratatouille or veggie burgers, but it can also be softened into spreads. There are more Sephardic uses of eggplant than I can list in one chapter, but for now I'll offer three options: 1) classic *babaghanoush*, 2) a Middle-Eastern-style eggplant salad that I invented one holiday when I was good and sick of my standard eggplant recipes, and 3) a Turkish moussaka-style main dish that I often make for holidays because it is not only delicious, but creates an elegant presentation for an inexpensive meat (it also happens to be Pesach-friendly). Give these a try and I guarantee you won't be alone in the kitchen with your eggplant for very long!

Classic Babaghanoush

1 large eggplant, rinsed and cut in half
3 tablespoons tehina
Juice of one lemon
2 cloves of garlic, run through a press
¾ teaspoon salt
½ teaspoon cumin (leave out if you don't like the taste of cumin)
2 tablespoons chopped fresh parsley or cilantro

Place eggplant cut sides down on a foil-lined baking sheet.

Now cook them under the broiler, several inches from the flame, for twenty minutes (you can also prick a whole eggplant with a fork and roast at 400 degrees for an hour, turning every twenty minutes or so). When the eggplant has cooled, scraped out the flesh, removing some of the seeds. Combine with the other ingredients and blend in your food processor or blender until smooth. Note: Many people like to add a tablespoon of mayonnaise, which will give a whiter color and smoother, richer texture.

Eggplant Spread

I large eggplant, peeled and cut into one-inch cubes
2 tablespoons olive oil
1 small onion, diced
1 clove garlic, minced
1 red pepper, cut into ½-inch dice
1 green or yellow pepper, diced
Salt, pepper, a pinch of sugar
½ teaspoon cumin
¼ teaspoon cayenne or hot paprika (or to taste)
¼ teaspoon turmeric
½ teaspoon paprika
Juice of ½ lemon
2 tablespoons chopped fresh parsley

Put the eggplant cubes into a vegetable steamer over a couple of inches of water in a pot and steam, covered, about fifteen-twenty minutes (until tender but not mushy). Heat oil in a saucepan and sauté the onion a few minutes until transparent; add the garlic and peppers and sauté a few minutes more, until vegetables have softened. Add the steamed eggplant cubes and the spices and combine gently over the heat for another few minutes (the eggplant cubes may start to get mushy and fall apart, that's fine—you're aiming for a chunky salsa-type texture). Serve slathered on challah or pita.

Moussaka Keftas

1 large eggplant, cut in 1/2-inch slices
Oil for frying
1 pound ground beef
1/3 cup breadcrumbs (use matzoh meal or leave out for Pesach)
1 egg, slightly beaten
Salt, pepper
1 teaspoon garlic powder
1 teaspoon paprika
3 tablespoons fresh chopped parsley
2 15-ounce cans tomato sauce
3 plum tomatoes, sliced thickly
2 tablespoons pine nuts, toasted (optional but they really help make the dish)

Sprinkle the eggplant slices with salt and let sit twenty minutes. Sponge off any moisture that collects with paper towels. Heat oil in a saucepan until very hot and fry the slices, turning once, until caramel-colored. Set aside.

Mix meat, bread crumbs, egg, salt, pepper, garlic powder, paprika, and one tablespoon of the parsley together in a bowl. Form patties like hamburgers and cook them in a saucepan with a little cooking spray (medium-high heat) until almost done (3-4 minutes a side). Place patties in a 9 x 13 pan (you may have to double up or use a slightly larger pan if you want them all in one layer). Pour the cans of tomato sauce over them. Now top each patty with one slice of eggplant and one slice of tomato. Bake at 350 degrees for half an hour; garnish with remaining parsley and pine nuts.

You will probably have some leftover eggplant slices. Mix them with a little chopped red pepper, a minced clove of garlic, some chopped parsley, and a little fresh lemon juice for a delicious salad!

Chapter 28

Sheesh — What Great Kebabs!

THERE WAS ONCE a time in the United States when Memorial Day signaled the moment where it was *de rigueur* for men and women of a certain social class to begin wearing white shoes— shoes which were then banished immediately after Labor Day. The advent of the summer season, anchored at each end by those two national holidays, initiated not only the wearing of white shoes, but another rather more plebian but infinitely less silly and more lovable American custom: the backyard barbecue.

Stoking up the grill has traditionally been a family affair. Women like it because all the kids and the mess are mostly outside the house, and because husbands who claim to not know where the kitchen is located are suddenly seized by some deep primordial instinct to roast raw meat over an open fire, staking control of the bounty and the fire. "I did the cooking," they boast, beaming with pride, while the wife—who knows all too well exactly where that kitchen is located—has just spent the entire afternoon inside the house making all the marinades and two salads and three side dishes (and, you guessed it, will return there later to take charge of the cleanup).

Oh well, at least barbecues are casual enough for paper plates, and it's a pleasure to see one's spouse humming old camp songs as his inner Boy Scout comes to the fore. And you have to admit that food that's been cooked outside over charcoal has a special flavor all of us love. It tastes good even when you don't do anything to jazz it up; in fact, it's really quite hard to ruin a decent piece of meat cooked on a grill.

Jews who come from the warm climates of the Levant and North Africa never had to wait for Memorial Day to barbecue, as if they had any idea what Memorial Day was. They availed themselves of outdoor grills during much of the year. "I remember in Morocco we were very food-centered, and everything always tasted so good," remembers my friend Miriam. "I think much of the reason was that we used to cook over coals outside a lot."

The opportunity to cook outside was especially handy *erev* Pesach, while the kitchen was being cleaned. All the food could be prepared and eaten outside! But in Brooklyn, when *erev* Pesach falls in March or early April, it's often still snowing outside (or at least freezing rain). It kind of discourages a girl from firing up the grill when she has to wear a scarf and mittens to turn the franks.

One of the Sephardic world's great contributions to cuisine is the shish kebab—chunks of meat and vegetables laced onto skewers and grilled to charred perfection. Shish kebab comes from a Turkish words meaning "roast meat" and "swords," so presumably we have the Turks to thank for this wonderful invention (along with the Ottoman Empire and Turkish baths). Shish kebab can be made of any kind of meat—in Arab countries you're more likely to find lamb than beef—which is usually marinated in oil and vinegar or lemon juice and spices to soften and flavor the meat before it is laid on the fire. Chicken also makes delicious shish kebob—it will cook faster than beef or lamb—and you can even make your shish kebab purely vegetarian for the macrobiotic members of the crowd, because even humble vegetables also taste better cooked over charcoal.

Shish kebab is traditionally served on a bed of rice or rice pilaf, although couscous also makes a nice accompaniment, with a hunk of pita bread. There are a few words of advice that go along with successful shish-kebabing: 1) it's handy to marinate the meat in a zip-lock bag, anywhere from one hour to overnight, in the fridge 2) if you are using wooden skewers instead of metal ones, soak them in water for half an hour before use to prevent them from burning 3) do not overload wooden skewers with very heavy chunks of meat or they will break in half, and 4) meat will release more easily from metal or wooden skewers if they are first sprayed with cooking spray.

So before you put away your white shoes and wheel the barbecue into the garage for the season, why not give it one last hurrah with some savory shish kebabs? Just be forewarned that these procedures carry a risk: namely, that all your neighbors will sniff the delicious scent of kebabs roasting on the grill and decide that maybe it's high time they hightailed it over to your place to ask how your summer went after all. . .

Ground Meat Kebabs

1 ½ pounds ground beef or lamb
1 chopped onion
1/3 cup fresh chopped parsley
½ teaspoon salt
½ teaspoon pepper
4 cloves garlic, minced or run through a press
1 teaspoon cumin

¼ teaspoon allspice
1 tablespoon lemon juice

Combine all ingredients well in a bowl. Form into about 20 round or oval patties and thread them three to a skewer; cook over a grill to taste (rare, well-done etc).

Beef Shish Kebab (adapted from Gilda Angel's *Sephardic Holiday Cooking*)

2 tablespoons vegetable oil
1 medium onion, grated
2 cloves garlic, minced or run through a press
Juice of 3 lemons (about 6 tablespoons)
3 pounds lean boneless beef shoulder or lamb shoulder, cut in 1 ½ inch cubes
Salt, pepper

Combine first four ingredients and marinate meat in this mixture 24 hours in the refrigerator, turning several times. Thread onto skewers, alternating with vegetables if desired (cherry tomatoes, mushrooms, green peppers, onions, etc). Grill until well done on all sides.

Chicken Shish Kebabs, Kurdish/Turkish style

2 pounds boneless skinless chicken thighs (baby chicken or pargiyot)
1 large clove of garlic
2 teaspoons salt
2 teaspoons ground coriander
1-1/2 teaspoons paprika
1 teaspoon oregano

1/2 teaspoon black pepper

1/3 teaspoon nutmeg

1/4 to 1/2 teaspoon hot red pepper flakes

1 teaspoon tomato paste (2 teaspoons ketchup can be substituted)

4 tablespoons lemon juice

2 tablespoons olive oil

Vegetables for grilling (e.g., tomatoes, long sweet peppers, mushrooms, small onions)

Olive oil and kosher salt for the vegetables

Za'atar or fresh parsley, for garnish (optional)

Cut the meat into pieces about 1-1/2 inches long, an inch wide and 1/2-inch thick. Place in a bowl. Put the garlic through a garlic press or mince finely. Add it along with the other ingredients (except the vegetables and the garnishes) to the chicken and mix well. Cover the bowl with plastic wrap or transfer the chicken and marinade to a zip-lock plastic food bag. Refrigerate for two hours or up to 24 hours, mixing the chicken from time to time for even seasoning.

Thread the chicken onto skewers, folding the chicken pieces in half. If flat, wide skewers are not used, stick a second skewer into each kebab, so the meat does not twist around. Make 12 kebabs, or six long ones.

Meanwhile coat the vegetables with olive oil and sprinkle with salt. Thread onto other skewers and grill along with the kabobs until charred. Serve meat and vegetables over rice and garnish with parsley or za'atar.

Vegetarian Shish Kebab

2 eggplants
2 zucchini
1 acorn or butternut squash
1 large onion
10 baby potatoes
10 cherry tomatoes
1 large green bell pepper
3 tablespoon olive oil
Kosher salt
Dash of dried thyme and parsley

Peel and cut the larger vegetables into chunks about the size of the baby potatoes and cherry tomatoes, so that all the vegetables are roughly the same size but big enough to be skewered. Toss with the olive oil, salt and spices to taste; cook over grill under tender.

Part Five

The Heart Of The Matter

Chapter 29

The Amazing Disappearing Family Dinner

My MOTHER-IN-LAW VISITED us some years ago, when our last child came into the world. Since she lives in Israel, her visits are no mere weekend stopovers. I usually figure on at least two months' worth of visit. It's the only way for her to really get to know her grandchildren and for them, in turn, to get to know her.

It's not always easy for people who are no longer young to change habitations, to sleep in strange beds and adjust to the rhythms of somebody else's household (especially when that household is on the noisy and cramped side). To her credit, my mother-in-law is a very good sport about putting up with lower levels of comfort than she would have at home. But the changes in culture, not only from one country to the other but from one generation to the next, throw her for more of a loop.

This really came out when it came to mealtimes. There was a vast difference between my family's modern American approach to mealtimes and my mother-in-law's old-fashioned Moroccan approach. You see, back in the days when my husband was a boy in Morocco, women *only* worked in the home, and opportunities for entertainment were limited. This meant that social life revolved around the home, with meals occupying center stage. Since even the most modest families had Arab maids, housewives had the extra time and where-withal available to fuss over such complicated, labor-intensive Moroccan *tours de force* as couscous, cooked salads, and pastries. You couldn't exactly run out and buy those things at the local takeout place in those days; any food that was kosher was necessarily produced in the home. The preparation of meals began early in the day and took hours of effort.

Between all the preparation involved, the high quality of the results and the lack of other sources of entertainment, meal-time had the status of a major event! In Morocco, as in many countries across the Atlantic, everything would shut down between noon and two o'clock, and everyone would go home for the main meal of the day. The table was laid out with a laundered tablecloth, napkins and porcelain; the family assembled, and a formal two or three-course meal ensued. French notions of table manners had replaced the old Arab table manners or lack thereof (i.e., eating with bread and one's fingers), and so everyone had to be careful to use the silverware correctly, eat noiselessly, and make appropriate conversation. Dining was nothing if not a *civilized* experience: a feast for the palate, a forum in which to exchange news and enjoy the company of others, and a place to put into practice refined behaviors that emphasized that eating is not only a biological experience, but a familial, social, and, through blessing the food, even spiritual one as well.

Now fast-forward to Brooklyn, thirty years later, and my mother-in-law's visit to our humble American abode. Location: my kitchen, a functional but inelegant space characterized by plastic tablecloths and paper plates. Time: five-thirty in the evening. Supper is almost ready, not quite; after all the baby woke up all of a sudden and needed to be fed, and then the diaper was dirty, and then the four-year-old spilled orange juice all over the floor. There are five kids pushing into the kitchen wanting to eat something NOW. My kitchen, like many in Brooklyn, would qualify in other locales as a nice-sized closet. I can fit four kids around the table, but not five, really. Forget about me-- I'll eat later, when things calm down, and I can eat without provoking major indigestion.

So the kids all start grabbing for food, with me yelling at them to sit down and wait their turn, and some of them already pouring themselves drinks and helping themselves to food that isn't even completely ready to serve. I run to intervene, and eventually everybody gets set up with supper in some shape or form, although one of the kids has gone off to the dining room to eat because there's no room left at the kitchen table for her and she doesn't have patience to wait for the next shift.

And then comes the chorus of commentaries:

"Not *meatballs*! I just had *meatballs* in school today! I don't wanna eat meat again!"

"I *hate* spaghetti! Why do you make spaghetti when you know I hate it!"

"I like spaghetti but I'm so *sick* of it! Can't you make something *new*?"

"Can I have a bowl of cereal for supper?"

The kids then proceed to consume the meal at a pace of about ninety miles an hour despite all the *kvetching*, and also despite a short series of time-outs for conflict resolution when there is an altercation over who spilled the salad and another over who drank juice from the wrong cup. Where am I, the parent, in all this? Trying to serve second helpings, wipe up spills, defuse further quarrels, and get more spaghetti out to the kid who went off to the dining room to eat.

My mother-in-law, taking in this scenario, is aghast. What

kind of way is this for a family to dine? Why wasn't the table nicely set before they all came trooping in? Why is the whole scene so disorganized, with one kid not even eating with the rest of them? Why aren't I sitting down with them? Why did the two-year-old run off before he finished all the food on his plate? Why is the four-year-old not using his fork?

She really had me there. To my great embarrassment, I had to admit she was absolutely right.

I told myself in self-defense that allowances have to be made in the months before and after a baby is born. Before I had the baby, I was so tired I was happy if I could just get dinner on the table in the evenings, and instilling proper dinner decorum was the least of my worries. Then after the baby was born I was struggling with postpartum fatigue plus the chaos of trying to integrate a newborn's schedule into everybody else's. But to be completely honest, things were not always so organized even when I didn't have the excuse of bringing a new life into the world.

And you know what? I didn't grow up with suppers like that either. I grew up in the middle-class suburban culture of enough years ago that my father always walked in the door punctually at six o'clock, and the whole family sat down to a more or less civilized supper not too long afterwards. My mother planned nice meals consisting of a protein, a vegetable and a starch; there was tea and dessert afterwards. Everyone stayed at the table until supper was over except my mother and me, who got up at intervals to clear. We all had to taste everything on our plates, and preferably finish it—no abandoning a half-finished plate (cf. the starving children in Asia), no whining about the choice of menu, and no abrupt exits (when was the last time you heard a kid ask his parents politely, "May I please be excused from the table?").

I began comparing notes with other women I know, and

soon realized that I am not alone in my suppertime woes. In this generation, very few women have husbands who walk in the door early enough to eat supper with the children—those poor beleaguered fellows are either working long hours, or working two jobs, or taking some evening class. Nobody's home at lunchtime either, so the only time anybody eats together as a family is on weekends. Thank G-d for that! And as the kids get older, the meals become even more fragmented. This son has baseball practice, this daughter stayed late for play practice, Mommy has to leave early to go to PTA. We have nice enough houses, but nobody ever seems to be home.

When my mother-in-law visited, the children's supper became a more organized affair. She helped with the cooking, so the food got done on time. She began pulling the kitchen table away from the wall in the evenings so we could fit all the kids around it at once, and helped me set the table properly before they tumbled in all at once for a meal. These were worthy changes, but I didn't always have the energy to keep them up after she left and I had to cope single-handedly. And then, before I knew it, the older kids had longer hours in school than the younger kids and we settled into eating in shifts anyway.

Yet I find myself left with the nagging, persistent feeling that something has been terribly lost with the disappearance of a formal family supper. Nowadays everybody is too much on the run to gather together regularly in the evenings for dinner. I read once that the genius of Ray Kroc, the founder of fast food, was to recognize that modern-day Americans never *dine*; they just "grab a meal." Today, apparently, we all have priorities other than taking time out to make and serve attractive, leisurely family meals.

But whatever the reason we find ourselves spending more and more time outside the home and less time inside, the bottom line is that nobody is ever home for meals all together, and this has produced a situation that is far from ideal. To begin with, there's not much incentive for a mother to lovingly slave over an elaborate supper if she knows the kids will gobble it up in three separate shifts of five minutes flat and the husband might end up eating on the outside anyway. What's the point of killing yourself in the kitchen—assuming you have the time in between work and errands and school pickups—when you know all too well the kids would be happier with a peanut butter sandwich, and when takeout food has become so cheap and available? You'd have to be an idiot to fuss over homemade meals when you can take that same money and send your twelve-year-old to the pizza store. Right?

Which leads us to the tremendous irony that, in a country where we have a greater quality and variety of food available to us than ever before in history (not to mention zillions of cookbooks and food magazines to tell us how to prepare it), so many of us seem to be subsisting mainly on potato chips, frozen pizza, and takeout chickens. We can't even be bothered to make our own tuna salad or coleslaw. Then, according to the food writers, for special occasions people go to trendy restaurants and order the latest culinary fashion: "comfort food!" Upscale versions of macaroni and cheese or meat loaf with mashed potatoes! People are so nostalgic for the old standbys, and yet so unwilling to go to the trouble of making them, that they are apparently willing to pay top dollar for dinners my mother never would have served to company.

Those of us who like to cook and appreciate good homemade cooking mourn the disappearance, more and more, of nourishing, chemically unaltered, tastier meals. But the main problem with the disappearance of the real family supper is not even so much the loss of wholesome home-cooked meals (although that is also a concern for mothers who do not believe pizza includes all four levels of the food pyramid). The problem is rather that when family dinner becomes a fragmented, rushed affair, eating becomes downgraded from a social, family event to a solitary refueling rather akin to filling up the gas tank of the car, and equally inspiring. Let's face it, the flavor of those home-cooked meals we all remember fondly didn't come only from Mom's expert touch in the kitchen; the flavor was enhanced by the fact that those meals were eaten *together*. If we don't eat together as a family, we lose golden opportunities for quality family time, and for the education of our children as well.

When the entire family makes a point of sitting down together for supper, the meal becomes more than a hasty restocking of the intestines so that we can go about the rest of our business unperturbed by hunger pangs. It becomes an event, the way my husband's boyhood meals in Morocco were an *event*: a moment of family time together with eating as the excuse. A family dinner is an opportunity for the inculcation of proper behavior and the exchange of news and ideas. It forces everyone to pause and relax together on a daily basis (emphasis on the *together*). It allows each family member the chance to report on his day to everybody else, to ask questions, to throw out topics for discussion. It helps structure the evening, because it puts everyone on the same timetable instead of having a supper that drags out from 4:30 for the little kids through 6:00 and/or 8:00 for the older kids and 9:00 for the husband.

Any mother who is accustomed to manning the ship alone on weeknights can tell you what a difference it makes when there are two parents present at a meal rather than one (imagine the possibilities for bedtime). Two grownups! Double authority! Double the pairs of hands available for serving, passing, cutting meat, enforcing time-outs! One person to serve and another to keep everybody seated firmly around the table making conversation! A mother harried with single-handedly getting a crew of youngsters fed and watered as well as preventing or salvaging kiddie food disasters has no time or presence of mind to concentrate on making genteel dinner conversation or perfecting her children's table manners.

The presence of a husband not only helps the meal run more smoothly, thanks to his additional adult participation and masculine authority, it even encourages them to eat better. I've noticed that my kids are much less whiney and capricious when my husband is around, somehow sensing that after a long day of work he's not going to give them much sympathy for not being in the mood for spaghetti tonight or not wanting to eat meatballs again. Besides, the very sight of the head of the household eating the supper and appearing to enjoy it lends the food a cachet it didn't have before. When we're all together, everybody eats more, and better, for now "grabbing some supper" has been upgraded to the status of "family powwow." Sometimes the kids will even try new things, to my great delight, since normally I find it quite a challenge to expand the borders of that very narrow chasm in between "What? That *again?*" and "What's *that?* I'm not eating *that* weird stuff!"

All of which leads to the conclusion that you'd be hard pressed to come up with a better way to strengthen the family unit than uniting regularly for mealtimes. We are all so busy these days, each person in his own orbit, that it would be tremendously helpful if we could pull all those satellites in for recalibrating at least once a day. We worry about alienated children, but some of those unhappy kids are not responsible for their own alienation; there was precious little family closeness in the first place. Contrary to popular belief, families do not run on auto-pilot; like marriages, they need nurturing and time to thrive. It would surely be harder to fall out of touch with our children if we saw them at an official family meal every day. It might help little problems from turning into big problems if we saw each other regularly enough to keep abreast of what other family members are up to, air our grievances, and give ourselves the chance to unwind at the end of the day with some pleasant family time, preferably including a few good laughs.

One last point: it should also be noted that our meals contain the oft-neglected potential to feel closer not only to our earthly family members, but, for those for whom religion is important, to the Creator as well. We may joke about good food being a "religious experience," but the truth is that it is important to appreciate food: appreciate that we have enough of it, appreciate that G-d made it tasty for us, appreciate that we are able to bless it. This is an equally important education to pass on to our children.

I am currently struggling to salvage some sort of family meals out of our unsynchronized schedules. Some nights it works, some nights it doesn't; there are still many weeks when a weekend meal or two are our only opportunity to eat together as a family. The "baby" is a big girl now, and the meals are somewhat less crazy now that everyone is a little bit older, a little more patient, and less prone to major food catastrophes. But I intend to persist in trying to keep us all together at mealtimes, knowing that at the very least "the family who eats together meets together." In an age where it's increasingly hard for families to stay together, we could start by staying together for supper.

Chapter 30

Brought Together by the Kitchen: A Tribute to my Moroccan Mother-in-Law

We know people bond when they share meals together, be it for Shabbos meals or dinners with friends. But people also bond when they prepare food together, even if they come from wildly different backgrounds.

Such was the case with my mother-in-law and me. We were so very different: She was an intelligent, proud, strong-willed woman who kept her home spotless as a museum and believed that children should mostly be seen and not heard. I was an easygoing American who got married straight out of graduate student life, where housekeeping was little more than a pesky footnote to the more compelling business of reading, writing and teaching. I'd been raised with a permissive American approach to childrearing. But four years after I got married, my in-laws decided to spend the month of Tishrei with us, and suddenly my mother-in-law and I found ourselves spending long hours in the kitchen together preparing meals for the chagim.

My in-laws traveled from Israel to Brooklyn on the heels of a family tragedy: My brother-in-law Jo had passed away in

190

Sivan at age 43, after struggling for years with a chronic illness. At the time, my husband and I were in Brooklyn, and I was a week overdue with my third child. With a baby imminent, my husband wasn't permitted to go sit shiva with his family in Israel, so he sat at home, a sad and lonely affair. (I still remember struggling to get out of bed at 6:30 a.m. to waddle to the corner to buy bagels, cream cheese and orange juice for the men who showed up for the morning minyan; Sephardim, unlike Ashkenazim, make a point of eating in a shiva house so they can make brachos *l'ilui nishmas* the niftar.)

I went into labor the morning my husband got up from sitting shiva. He took the ritual walk around the block and then drove me straight to the hospital, where I delivered a baby boy a few hours later. Eight days later, the baby received his deceased uncle's name at the bris. When they told my mother-in-law, she fainted from emotion.

A couple of months later, my in-laws announced that they'd decided to come spend Tishrei with us. After losing their beloved oldest son, they needed a change of scene, and meeting the new grandson who bore his name was an additional draw.

At that point, I'd been married just over four years, but I hadn't spent all that much time together with my in-laws. They'd come in for our wedding, but I was a busy kallah, and my mother-in-law, ever occupied with cooking for the family, always shooed me out of the kitchen. We'd spent a Pesach together in France, but she and my sisters-in-law cooked while I chased after two toddlers.

While I was warmly welcomed into the family, my mother-in-law, whom we called Mamy Gisele, and I came from very different worlds and generations. I always suspected she might have enjoyed an easier connection to a girl of her own background (although I definitely rated higher than the sister-in-law who converted). Now we were almost haphazardly tied together by my husband and children.

I was a girl from suburban America, who'd been raised with lots of freedom (probably way too much, I would say today). I was sent to college because feminism, still a new trend, pushed young women of my ilk to pursue some sort of brilliant career. We were told, "Who wants to be a housewife? Any ditz could clean a house and watch little children." Little did I know that raising little children would be the toughest job I'd ever love, and that running a home, when done well, actually requires substantial skill sets...

My mother-in-law, by contrast, had grown up in an Arab country. She'd dreamed of becoming a nurse, but her parents absolutely forbade it, saying that the hospitals were full of Arabs and were no place for a Jewish girl. They apprenticed her to a well-regarded tailor, and she ended up marrying him. Once married, it would have been unthinkable for her to work outside the home, although she sometimes helped her husband with his business. Instead, her job was to prepare abundant, delicious Moroccan meals and work with the maids to keep the house immaculate. (My own mother would never had had the idea to hire a maid; she grew up as the daughter of poor immigrants who were grateful to simply have something to cook). The domestic arts weren't just a job for Mamy. They were her pride.

With a Moroccan daughter-in-law, Mamy Gisele would have known what to expect, shared a mentality, shared more language (I could handle the French but not the Arabic, and I was quite sure when my husband's lapsed into Arabic that they were either talking about me or saying things they didn't want me to hear). But there was one advantage to being an unknown quantity, a newcomer: unlike my sisters-in-law, who came from Morocco and had their own ways of doing Moroccan food--and didn't want to be told how to do it better--I was a blank slate. I had no pride in my ability to produce a good couscous or matbucha, because I knew zilch. So I submitted myself as a willing apprentice.

Now my mother-in-law would be in my house for a month and a half, and despite our differences, we shared our love of my husband, children and cooking. I might have spent years pursuing an academic career, but I was also the daughter of a mother who liked to cook, and had picked up that love of the kitchen. The chagim were upon us and there were endless Shabbat and yom tov meals to prepare, and—imagine that!--the rest of the family had the nerve to expect regular meals when it *wasn't* chag. I took on the job of sous-chef, and as I worked I learned how Mamy made Moroccan fish, salads, chicken, keftas, even cookies. In between the peeling, chopping and simmering, she related a lot of family lore, so I learned a lot of family history, heard a lot of old stories.

The activity was good for her, even if her knees ached after a long day of cooking. It kept her mind off her recent loss, at least sometimes. In the same way parents of teens are advised to carry out sensitive conversations while engaged in another activity, like driving, my mother-in-law and I spoke about painful experiences too, our eyes trained on garlic and peppers, tears running not just from the onions. In some respects it was beneficial that I was a newcomer to the family, not tainted by past misunderstandings or history. I was Switzerland, neutral territory—less fiery, opinionated, and animated than the Moroccans she knew, but a soft cushion for her loss, a loss whose depth I only fully understood years later when I lost an adult child of my own.

I don't know how we would have bonded if we simply sat around a table with our hands folded, drinking tea, two strangers searching to make conversation. Cooking together allowed us to get to know each other in a natural fashion, through a shared, purposeful activity. I didn't just learn Moroccan cooking; I learned a whole family, a whole culture. As the years passed, and my father-in-law passed away, she continued to come to us for long stretches to spend holidays or attend simchas. Each time, our exchanges expanded and deepened, as did my store of Moroccan recipes.

Today, Mamy Gisele is no longer with us, but sometimes I miss her presence beside me in the kitchen when I simmer fish or make the little orange-scented, chocolate-filled rolls my children adored.

When you share food, you share your lifestyle, culture, tastes, family tradition. As I absorbed Moroccan cooking, the gulf between Marrakech and Brooklyn narrowed. Even better, we forged ties of understanding and love between two strangers who suddenly found themselves bound together as family.

Chapter 31

A Delicate Balance: The Mitzvah of Receiving Guests

Reb Yosef was an Iranian man, no longer young, who used to stop by our house from time to time. My husband had met him at a wedding, where he was collecting money to buy insulin for his sick mother in Iran. He felt an affinity for us because our last name, Ben-Shushan, indicates that my husband's family originally came from the same part of Iran that he was from, and because he enjoyed speaking the French he had learned at the *Alliance Francaise* in Iran with us. He would come to the house, accept a cup of tea and something to eat, take a donation to help his mother and leave. We never knew when he would show up and were never clear where exactly he lived or how he kept himself fed and clothed.

On his last visits, he complained of feeling sick and said the doctors said something was very wrong with his liver. We tried to trace him subsequently, but without any success. We only know that he suddenly disappeared from our lives, and we never knew for sure if he was who he said he was, or a charlatan, or perhaps Elijah the Prophet (who is reputed to appear unexpectedly in people's lives) in one of his many manifestations.

In order to show his gratitude whenever he enjoyed our hospitality, Reb Yosef, who was a Kohen, would give us a blessing before he left, addressing me by my Hebrew name. "Thank you very much, Mrs. Bracha," he would tell me. "I bless you that your house should always be open like the house of Avraham and Sara, that you should always have many, many guests and give them kindness like you give me." Then he would say *birkat haKohanim*, the priestly blessing, over the head of the baby and the other kids before he departed. I was never quite sure how I was supposed to respond, especially since I never knew exactly who he was, but I figured a *bracha* couldn't hurt and did my best to accept it with good grace.

In recent years, I have often thought about Reb Yosef, usually with the eerie conviction that his *bracha* must have wielded some supernatural influence, because ever since his departure our house has never ceased to be open to guests for very long. There always seems to be somebody camping out in the kids' playroom or popping up from overseas or sent by a friend ("Why don't you try the Bensoussans—they always have people over"). My husband and I are both sociable types who are happy enough to be of service where we can; however, I have noticed over time that this is a mitzvah with as many different faces as our guests.

The Torah describes how Avraham roused himself after his circumcision on a particularly hot day in the desert, to implore three guests to abide with him a moment and enjoy the best his household had to offer. The kind of self-sacrifice shown by Avraham in order to do the mitzvah of receiving guests is way beyond the capacity of most of us today. But we do accept sacrifices on a smaller scale when we open our homes to guests.

I have seen both extremes when it comes to *hachnasat*

orchim, the mitzvah of receiving guests. I know families who almost never take Shabbat guests, valuing their privacy, family time, and hard-earned hours of rest. Not everyone is at ease with guests, particularly total strangers, or has energy to make conversation on a Friday night when tired and looking forward to an early bedtime. At the opposite extreme are families who undertake every week to receive six, ten, even fifteen guests at their table. There's a family in my neighborhood that is known for taking practically a minyan every week of "older singles" into their home—not ebullient young people in town for a *shidduch*, but middle-aged, sometimes eccentric folks who have been alone for many years and have no one else they can count on for a steady invitation.

I know families of Lubavitch outreach workers who also receive small crowds week after week in their homes, people of every conceivable size, color and orientation, and do it always with unflagging enthusiasm and love for their fellow Jew. The wives in these families deserve tremendous credit for the institutional quantities of food they cheerfully prepare, not to mention clean up. Instead of sitting tranquilly during the meal, they're constantly popping up to serve or clear, and there's no guarantee of snuggling into bed early on a Friday night. The expense is also far from negligible when preparing for a small army. I have only the deepest admiration for such people, wondering when they manage to rest when every Shabbat is dedicated to serving others!

I have to admit that when, in the early years of my marriage, we started inviting guests, my motives were based more on selfishness than altruism. I would get bored being stuck home all Shabbat with little babies, so it livened up the day for me if a new face came to participate in our meals. Physically, the whole enterprise was less taxing back then; there were quite a few less of us then, and the kids who were there did little more than mouth a piece of challah and fall asleep in the highchair. We could have four or five guests and still not be feeding more than seven people. Now we are more than seven people all by ourselves, *bli ayin hara,* and many of us consume serious quantities of food, so if we invite five or six guests my Shabbat preparations resemble catering for a small wedding.

But the more delicate issue involves the children, who no longer fall asleep in the highchair but who come home with reams of parsha questions, Torah tidbits and personal news to give over. As the family and tuitions have grown, my husband is more frequently obliged to be absent on weekday nights to make ends meet, meaning that Shabbat meals are one of our few windows of opportunity for pan-family communication and relaxation. When there's a horde of guests, some of whom may also be hungry for attention, it's not so easy for a seven-year-old to get his two cents in.

Not only that, but after a certain age the kids have the nerve to actually start having opinions about people. "Oh, not *him* again," groaned my son as few weeks ago upon learning that a certain person was coming for Shabbat. "All he does is shmooze and shmooze with Papa and then I'm so bored!" So I then tried to give over something I've come to realize myself over the years: sometimes you take in guests because it's a pleasure, and sometimes you do it because it's a mitzvah. But try telling that to a kid who hasn't seen much of his father all week. He may understand it intellectually, but what it feels like is, "The guest is more important than me." So the wise parent tries to make sure that the child gets his piece of the pie, as it were, as much as everyone else.

The personal qualities of the guests have a lot to do with the children's willingness to have them join our Shabbat table. As Rabbi Dessler points out in his famous collection of essays *Michtav M'Eliayahu (Strive for Truth!),* in this life there are givers and takers. While by definition a guest is someone who takes, who accepts hospitality from you, a guest who is himself giving by nature will show his or her appreciation in some way: a bouquet of flowers before Shabbat, a bottle of wine, some candy for the kids. Heaven knows we as hosts don't actually *need* these things, after a day or two of intensive shopping and cooking. But the gesture of appreciation is always taken to heart. Even a compliment on the food is a gift to the wife who has spent time trying to make it nice. I have a particular soft spot for guests who take time to show some interest in the children, so they don't get bored or feel themselves to be invisible (not to mention disappearing from the table in frustration).

The "takers," on the other hand, are those needy people who dominate the conversation with their personal issues, who usurp a husband's attention so that the wife and children are left abandoned at the other end of the table, and who don't say thank you when it's all over. Some guests are basically well-intentioned but insensitive, such as the overly enthusiastic yeshiva student who can't wait to regale everyone with his latest Torah insights, meanwhile failing to notice that half of the table is getting an early start on their Shabbat naps. Then there are some singles and/or new returnees to Judaism who, in their earnestness to share the details of their life struggles with a sympathetic ear, sometimes forget that much of their audience is underaged and only allowed to attend "G" rated conversations.

While guests like these can put a strain on a family's Shabbat time together, the truth is that they also need a place to eat and someone to talk to. Those are the cases where I sometimes feel G-d is trying to test me: "You said you liked to take in guests, as a mitzvah? Ha! See if you're still so eager to keep doing it when it means giving up family time to spend Friday evening with So-and-So!" It takes no small effort to maintain

Barbara Bensoussan

the balance between time for the family and time for guests, and between hosting guests who are a pleasure to receive and hosting guests who are less easy yet equally in need of a place to go.

Reb Yosef's *bracha* has brought us many interesting people over the course of time, and I hope we have been able to be helpful to them without also neglecting the needs of our children. We live in a country of prosperity, where even poor people rarely go hungry, so it is hardly difficult materially to share our food with a fellow Jew. But we also live in a time of great emotional and spiritual hunger, where the warm family ambiance and Torah insights of a Shabbat table are deeply important for so many people who are lost or alone. May we be granted the strength and the means to fulfill this mitzvah to the best of our abilities, whether the Shabbat table can hold one or a dozen courses of food and one or a dozen guests.

Chapter 32

When the Priceless Gets Priced Out

I HAD a blast of nostalgia recently when I read an article by commentator Peggy Noonan about an attempt to reinstate S & H Green Stamps, those sheets of stamps we used to receive at the grocery store and redeem for items like toasters and coffee machines. Ms. Noonan wistfully remembers pasting stamps in the S & H books with her mother, and the way slowly filling up the books made for an exercise in patience and discipline. But she was not very optimistic that Green Stamps will go over in the twenty-first century. "Once we had more time than money in America," she writes. "Now we have more money than time. That is the difference between your child's America and yours."

"More money than time". . .the phrase caught in my mind and reverberated for days. It rang so true. Not that I am rolling in money, mind you; usually by the end of the month I look at the checkbook and start to hyperventilate. It's rather that today's economic pressures and general mindset so often lead us to evaluate all our pursuits in terms of their dollar value. Using time in ways that don't bring in money, or taking time away from bringing in money, gets looked at as a waste or an indulgence, rather than something that may have essential (albeit intangible) value for one's quality of life or spiritual growth. It's an issue of particular relevance to women, because as more and more of us work outside the home, those unpaid, time-consuming activities we did in previous centuries suddenly seem to diminish in value when compared to activities that bring home a paycheck.

Take the example of baking challah. It's more expensive to buy challah than to make it; for the price of one bakery challah one can buy a bag of flour than will yield six. But if a woman works and makes thirty or forty dollars an hour, then she can more than afford to absorb the extra costs of store-bought bread. She can sit at her desk and never have to sweat from a hot oven, wash out a mixer, or aggravate her varicose veins. It makes an ordinary balabusta feel downright foolish for knocking herself out when it's so much easier to run to the corner and buy the stuff. Her only consolation is the thought that at least if she bakes challah herself she can be sure there are no suspicious chemicals in it to give it a longer shelf life.

And yet there are considerations other than saving time or money, or even avoiding nasty food additives. What price the taste of freshly baked homemade challah, or the heavenly smell that fills a house as it bakes? What price the knowledge that our valiant balabusta took the *terumah* [a portion of dough we're halachically required to separate] herself, rather than counting on the bakery to do it for her? What price the appreciation of her family, not to mention the example to the children that Shabbos is worth a mother's best efforts?

By the same logic, one can ask why any woman would bother to stay home scrubbing out the bathtub and changing dirty diapers when she could hire a cleaning lady and a babysitter to do the job for a grand total of perhaps fifteen dollars an hour. If she goes out to work, she could easily make twice that amount and never have to scrub her own bathtub. From the point of view of pure economics, parenting one's own child makes less sense than working at a job that pays substantially more than what the babysitter makes. For many women, the margin of profit that remains after the babysitter and cleaning lady have been paid is important enough to make working outside the home an uncontested necessity.

But each family has to evaluate its priorities. Some "needs" —rent, food, etc., are clearly nonnegotiable; others are more debatable. And children have needs as well, which can only be "paid" for by a mother's investment of time with them. The early years of a child's life never come back, and I can tell you from experience they go by very fast. Who is going to leave those indelible first impressions, that first orientation to Jewish values, in the child's mind? We have to be very careful when we weigh the tradeoffs between creating solid bank accounts and creating solid kids. And since we've all gotten so used to considering things in terms of their dollar value, consider this: skimping on being there for our children in the short term can turn out to be very expensive in the long term if we end up having to call in psychotherapists and tutors to repair the damages later down the road.

When we, especially women, exchange our time at home for time outside making money, we run the risk that the home will become reduced to a place where everybody comes to only at night to wolf down a takeout meal and roll into bed. I know people who work hard to afford their gorgeous homes, but they're never home to enjoy them (ditto the women with beautiful custom kitchens who never cook). A vicious cycle gets created where the more we women work, the more we need to run out and buy the things we otherwise would have made ourselves at home. Then we need to go out and make yet more

203

money to support our expensive habits of outsourcing meals, repairs and services from other people. When we're not at work, we're running around buying things. Then we wonder why so many of our youth are spending all their time running around on the streets. Why should they stay home if nobody's there, physically or emotionally?

Both our quality of life and our spirituality suffer when we seek to buy on the outside rather than personally invest ourselves in the areas that are so fundamental to our lives: food, an orderly house, clothing, Shabbats and holidays. For example, I know people whose "celebration" of Chanukah means telling the housekeeper to pop a package of frozen latkes in the oven for the kids. That certainly avoids the problems of scraped knuckles, dirty pots, and potato starch turning brown on the counters. But frozen latkes are only the weakest approximation to the real thing (my apologies to frozen latke manufacturers), and more importantly, there is a message being sent that the holiday is not important enough to warrant scraped knuckles and an evening spent next to a frying pan. Likewise, these days a mother has a choice between buying a Purim costume for her child or making one herself. But a child's eyes will not shine in the same way over a chintzy store-bought costume as they will over an original "creation' Mommy stayed up all night sewing, nor will he or she get to bask in the exclamations of the neighbors: "Your mommy *made* that! *Wow!*" The message registers: look how important Mommy thinks I am. Look how important Purim is in our family.

I do not mean to advocate that every Jewish woman must stay at home chained to her stove and sewing machine. A Jewish mother's primary job is the raising of her children, to bring them up in the path of Torah, rather than to keep the furniture immaculate or make her own muffins from scratch every morning. But even the job of bringing up children as faithful Jews cannot be accomplished if she does not allow herself the time to create a joyful, inspiring Jewish home life for them. As a psychologist once said, there is no way to have "quality time" with children unless a minimum of "quantity time" has been spent (this applies equally to our relationships with spouses, friends, even Hashem). And the education she gives will not inspire them unless it is clear that she herself is enthusiastic about Judaism and is willing to put the best of her time and energy into the practice of it, in whatever way is most appropriate to her own particular talents and inclinations. While it is often necessary in today's world to spend money rather than time, and to take shortcuts wherever we can, I believe that ultimately there are no shortcuts when it comes to creating truly warm, nostalgia-laden Jewish memories in the mind of a child.

It used to be very hard to be Jewish; in our generation, at least in the urban centers of America, it's a pleasure. We have an explosion of choices in every aspect of Jewish living; we don't need to exert any outstanding self-sacrifice to obtain kosher food, keep Shabbos, dress in Jewish ways. So our challenge today, the least we could do in fact, is to avoid taking it all for granted and instead to use our new opportunities and prosperity to do mitzvahs with as much enthusiasm as we can muster. If our children see that we show no personal investment or willingness to sacrifice in the way we carry out a Jewish lifestyle, they will absorb that Judaism is not truly important to us, not something we need to strive for, but rather a bunch of rules we follow out of social pressure. Their youthful need for ideals will become frustrated and turn into cynicism and disillusionment if they see that Judaism has become just another commodity to buy, as we go about buying our food for Shabbos and yom tov, buying kosher food for Pesach and costumes for Purim, buying babysitters and tutors to bring up and educate our children. I truly doubt Hashem intended our Judaism to be something we should buy rather than create. When we spend time and energy putting ourselves into creating beautiful Jewish Shabbosim, holidays, and home lives in general, we become partners with Hashem in creating holiness. We grow ourselves, and enjoy observance more fully. We inspire our children to want to do the same.

I don't think I'd collect Green Stamps if they came back, for the same reason I rarely use coupon—usually it's not worth my time. But I certainly share nostalgia for a time when Americans had more time than money: time to create things, time to preserve things instead of throwing them out and buying new ones; time to sit on the front steps and chat with neighbors in the summer instead of running out on errands or sitting in front of a computer screen making the latest trade. In the Jewish world, it has become more difficult, but more important, to reserve time for Jewish family life. There's not much point in paying all that money for yeshiva tuition if the child comes home to a vacant Jewish home and home life. Money can be earned and lost and earned again; it is replaceable. But time is not. If we spend enough time improving the quality of Jewish family life, we'll end up with bonuses much more lasting than Green Stamps: the continuation of the legacy that was entrusted to us at Sinai, and Jewish *nachas* from our children.

About the Author

Barbara Bensoussan has been a journalist for Jewish newspapers and magazines for over 25 years, and received two Simon Rockower Awards for her work. She has edited and ghostwritten numerous books and memoirs, but her most satisfying--and creatively challenging--work has been her novels and culinary memoir.

She lives in Brooklyn with her husband, Ariel, in a not-very-empty nest, as most of their children and grandchildren live nearby and show up frequently to make sure she abandons her computer on a regular basis. When not writing, or lost in a good read, you can probably find her in the kitchen turning out homemade challah or Moroccan specialties.

barbarabensoussan.com

 instagram.com/barbarabensoussan

Also by Barbara Bensoussan

Pride and Preference

A New Song

Made in the USA
Las Vegas, NV
12 January 2025

16259697R00128